CW00590049

village classified
- restricted distribution -

Due to operational security, this manual is for
the specific use of personnel posted to
Prototype: Village. Any unauthorised circulation
of this reference guide is to be reported to
Village security immediately.

the prisoner™

The Village Files

tim palgut

TITAN BOOKS

THE PRISONER: THE VILLAGE FILES
1 80423 597 7

Published by
Titan Books
A division of
Titan Publishing Group Ltd
144 Southwark St
London
SE1 0UP

First edition February, 2003
10 9 8 7 6 5 4 3 2 1

Six of One is the official appreciation society for The Prisoner. They can be contacted at:
www.theprisonerappreciationsociety.com or Box 66, Ipswich, IP2 9TZ.

Did you enjoy this book? We love to hear from our readers. Please e-mail us at:
readerfeedback@titanemail.com or write to Reader Feedback at the above address.
Be seeing you!

To subscribe to our regular newsletter for up-to-the-minute news, great offers and competitions,
email: **titan-news@titanemail.com**
Titan Books are available from all good bookshops or direct from our mail order service.
For a free catalogue or to order, phone **01536 76 46 46** with your credit card details or contact
Titan Books Mail Order, Unit 6, Pipewell Industrial Estate, Desborough, Kettering, Northants NN14 2SW,
quoting reference TP/VF.

A CIP catalogue record for this title is available from the British Library.

Printed in Italy

acknowledgements

Grateful thanks to the following people for encouragement and assistance:

My parents for believing in this project.
Patrick McGoohan for creating *The Prisoner*.
My high school instructor for introducing me to *The Prisoner*.
Jack Shampan, Art Director of *The Prisoner* who created such a distinctive look for the Village.
Adam Newell my editor for advice and support.
David Hughes for advice, support, and connecting me with the right people.
David Schmidt for computer assistance back in the early days of the book, and general technical advice.
Heather Murray for much technical advice.
Van Wilson for more computer assistance.
Sherman Arnold Jr. and Lisa Foley-Smythe for even more computer assistance in the book's formative stages.
Roger Earl and Fredrik Thorsen for video assistance.
Scott Witmer for general advice.

well
come

village tenet and mandate

The Village is Power Control. The community must be sustained to avoid the
erratic tendencies of individuals in society. We must maintain the status quo.
It must be remembered that humanity is not humanised without force, and
that errant children must be brought to book with a smack on their backsides.
By use of attrition, clandestine preventative maintenance and possibly even
plausible deniability, the system of values held by certain extraneous
members of society can be prioritised into a civilised manner. These self-
appointed sentinels of individualism have delusions of adequacy; it is
common knowledge that individuals are all the same, and must be stamped
out and abolished. The community is at stake, and we have the means to
protect it. Power Control is the Village.

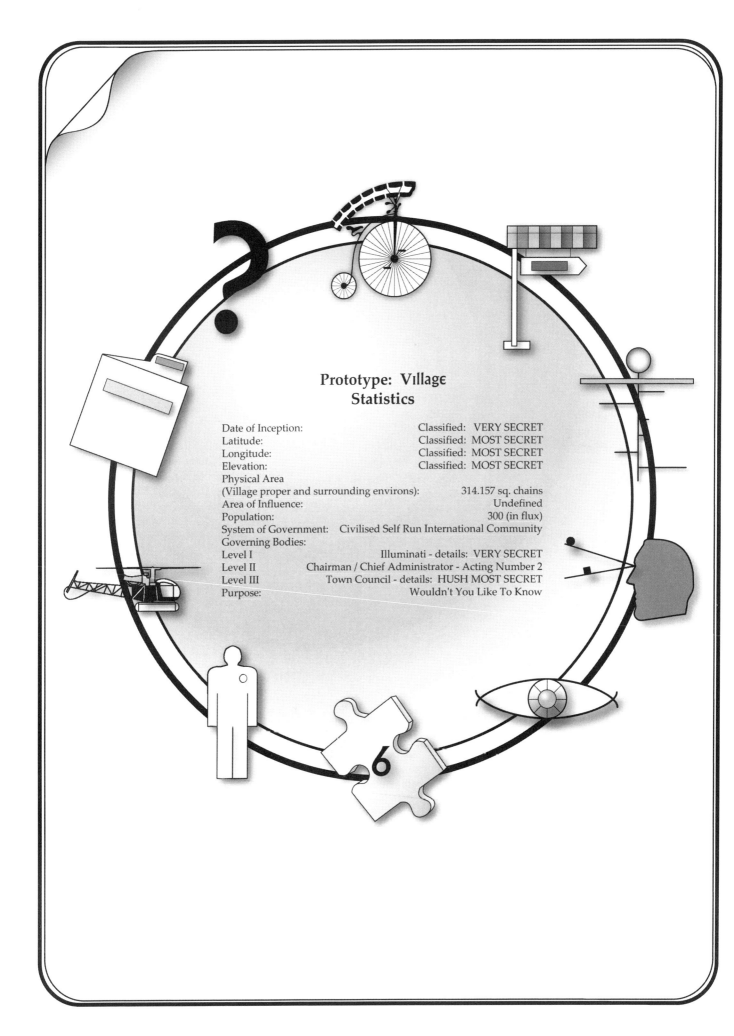

Prototype: Village
Statistics

Date of Inception:	Classified: VERY SECRET
Latitude:	Classified: MOST SECRET
Longitude:	Classified: MOST SECRET
Elevation:	Classified: MOST SECRET
Physical Area (Village proper and surrounding environs):	314.157 sq. chains
Area of Influence:	Undefined
Population:	300 (in flux)
System of Government:	Civilised Self Run International Community
Governing Bodies:	
Level I	Illuminati - details: VERY SECRET
Level II	Chairman / Chief Administrator - Acting Number 2
Level III	Town Council - details: HUSH MOST SECRET
Purpose:	Wouldn't You Like To Know

within...

power control

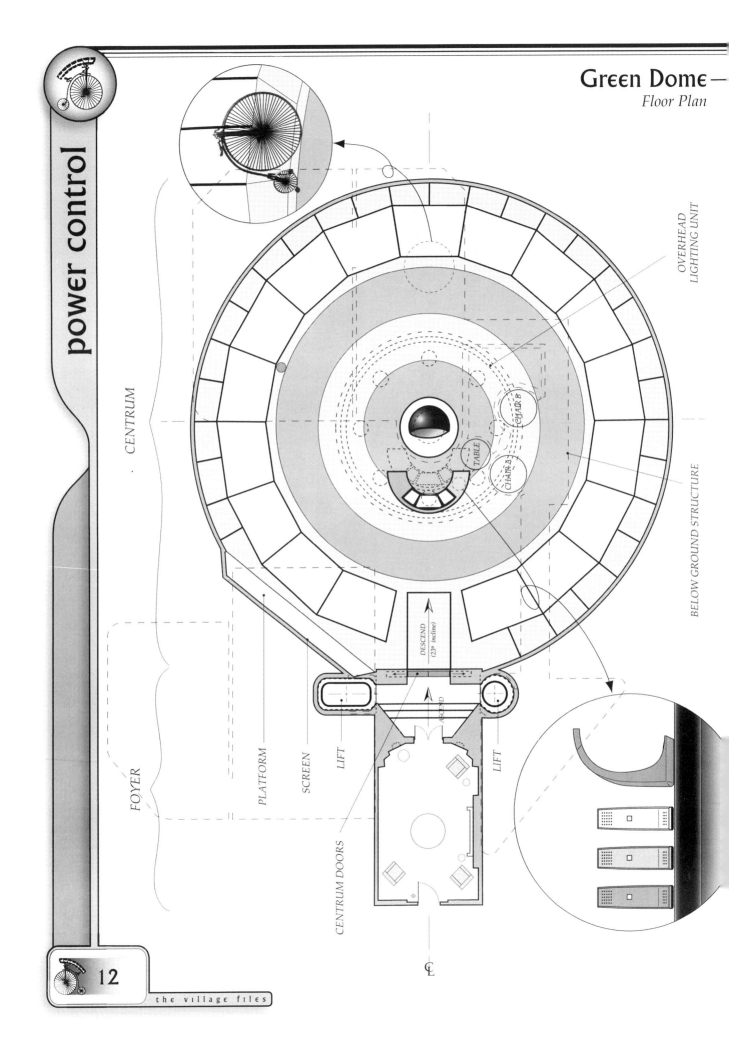

Green Dome—
Floor Plan

OVERHEAD
LIGHTING UNIT

CENTRUM

BELOW GROUND STRUCTURE

CHAIR B

CHAIR A

TABLE

DESCEND
(23° incline)

ASCEND

FOYER

PLATFORM

SCREEN

LIFT

LIFT

CENTRUM DOORS

C↓L

Green Dome

Number 2's Quarters - Floor Plan

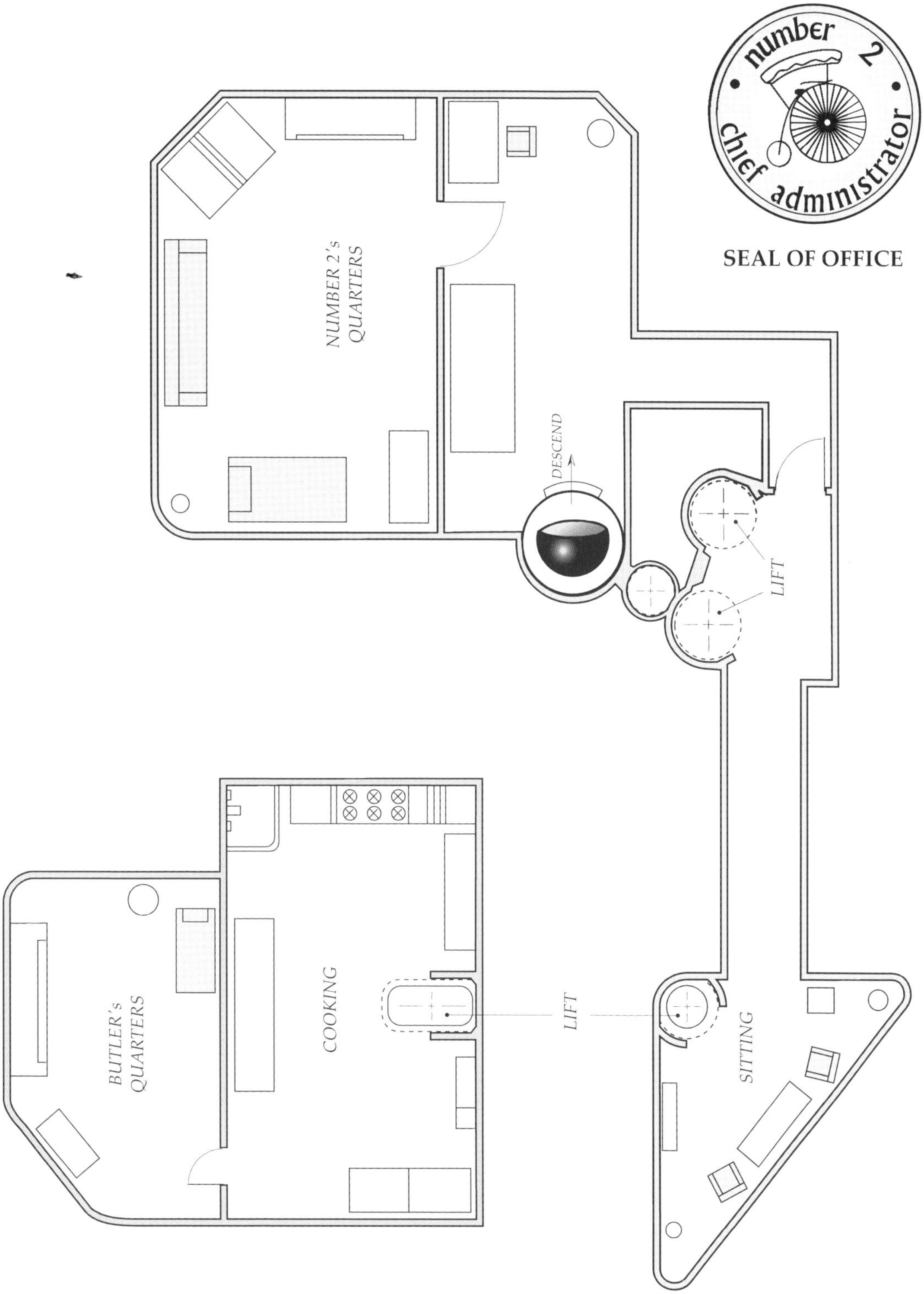

NUMBER 2's QUARTERS

DESCEND

LIFT

LIFT

BUTLER's QUARTERS

COOKING

LIFT

SITTING

number 2

chief administrator

SEAL OF OFFICE

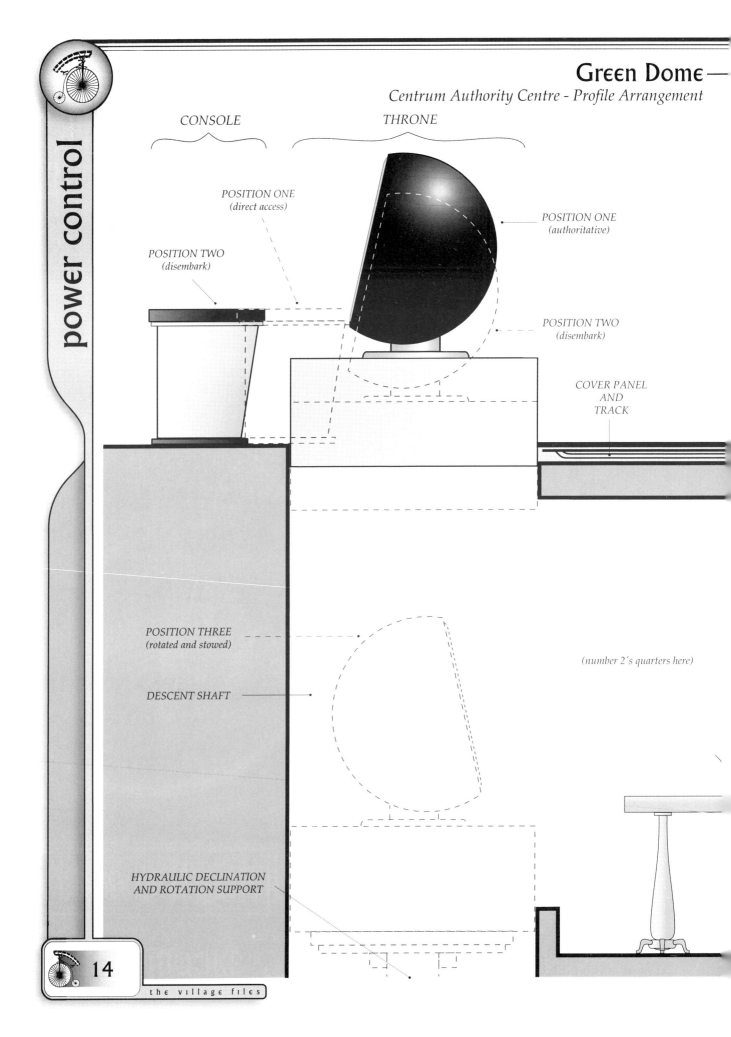

power control

CONSOLE

THRONE

POSITION ONE
(direct access)

POSITION ONE
(authoritative)

POSITION TWO
(disembark)

POSITION TWO
(disembark)

COVER PANEL
AND
TRACK

(number 2's quarters here)

POSITION THREE
(rotated and stowed)

DESCENT SHAFT

HYDRAULIC DECLINATION
AND ROTATION SUPPORT

Green Dome

Centrum Authority Console - General Arrangement

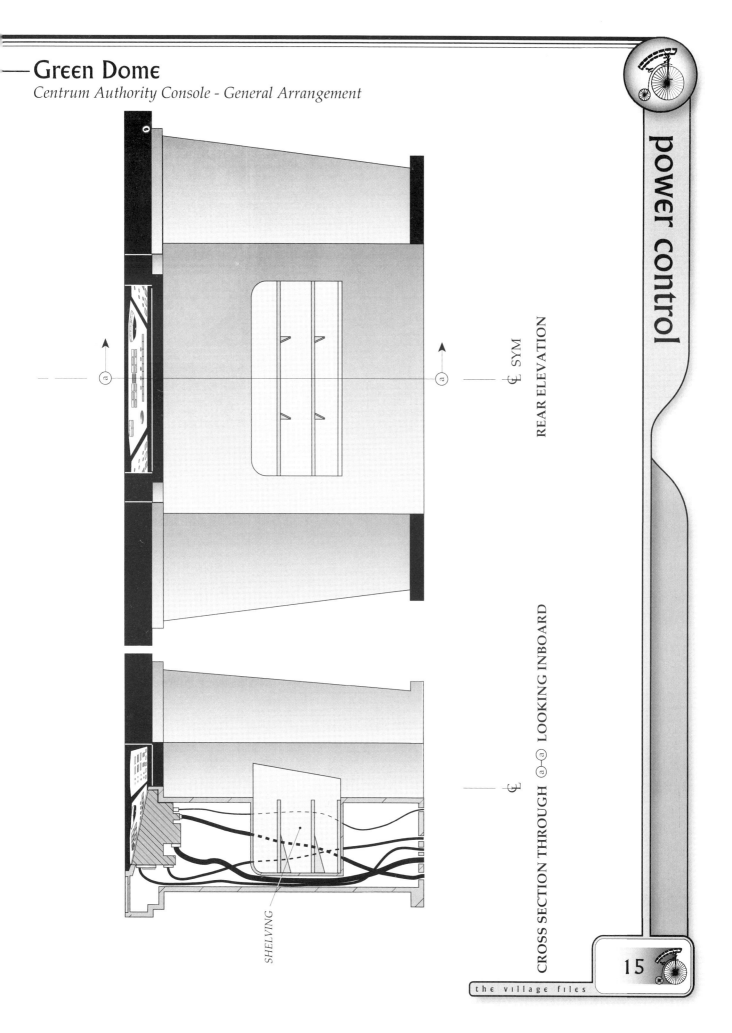

REAR ELEVATION

₵ SYM

SHELVING

₵

CROSS SECTION THROUGH (a)-(a) LOOKING INBOARD

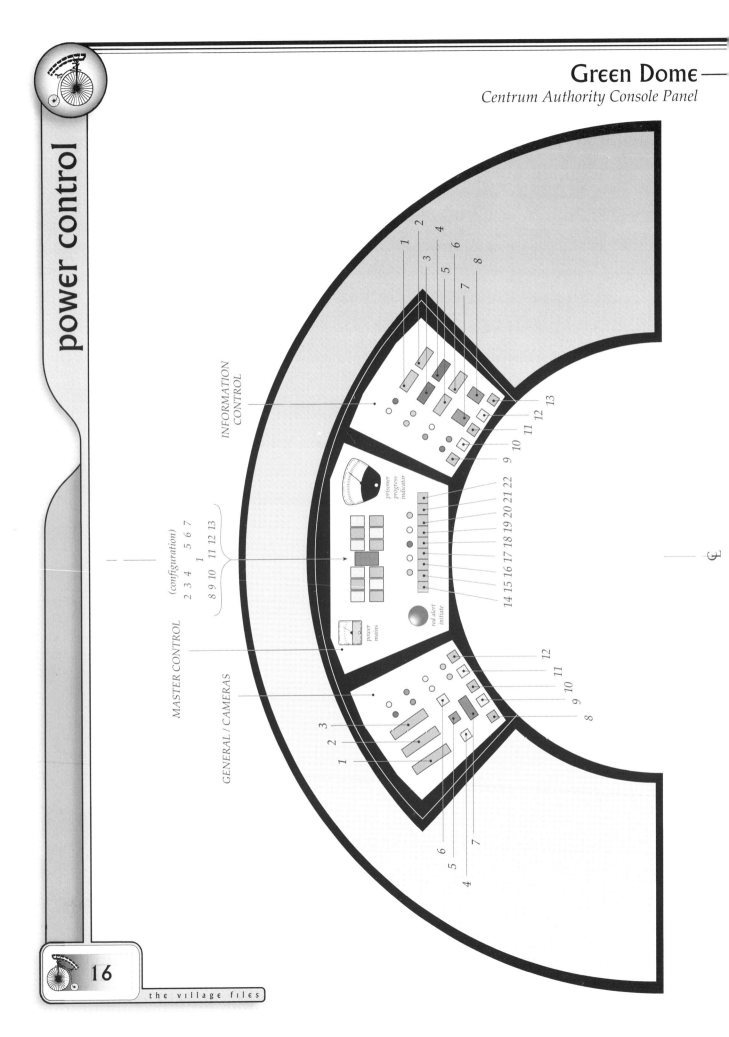

power control

INFORMATION CONTROL

MASTER CONTROL

(configuration)

2 3 4   5 6 7
        1
8 9 10 11 12 13

GENERAL / CAMERAS

prisoner progress indicator

power mains

red alert initiate

—Green Dome
Centrum Authority Centre - Information

General / Cameras Panel

- General Controls Mode -
1 Phone activation toggle.
2 Screen curtain.
3 Rover control.
4 Retrieve data / image from control room.
5 Record on / off toggle.
6 Send data / image to control room.
7 Mode toggle.
8 Tape stop.
9 Tape play.
10 Tape pause.
11 Tape rewind.
12 Tape fast forward.

- Camera Controls Mode -
1 Preprogrammed camera / data input.
2 Screen curtain.
3 Preprogrammed camera / data input.
4 Preprogrammed camera / data input.
5 Preprogrammed camera / data input.
6 Preprogrammed camera / data input.
7 Mode toggle.
8 Lock camera to subject.
9 Camera image process. (vector enhancement, computer aging, infrared, x-ray, electromagnetic, video separation)
10 Camera zoom. (-)
11 Camera zoom. (+)
12 Screen off.

Master Control Panel

1 Call control room.
2 Custom modify and execute.
3 Custom modify and execute.
4 Custom modify and execute.
5 Custom modify and execute.
6 Custom modify and execute.
7 Custom modify and execute.
8 Custom modify and execute.
9 Custom modify and execute.
10 Custom modify and execute.
11 Custom modify and execute.
12 Custom modify and execute.
13 Custom modify and execute.
14 Throne position 3.
15 Throne position 2.
16 Throne position 1.
17 Centrum doors manual override.
18 Chair A up / down toggle.
19 Chair B up / down toggle.
20 Direct camera lock on preprogrammed prisoner.
21 Public announcement activation.
22 Spotlight activation.

Information Control Panel

1 Page advance.
2 Page return.
3 Information processor.
4 Step advance.
5 Data expand.
6 Information backup to mainframe.
7 Table up.
8 Table down.
9 Retrieve files list.
10 Input / output toggle.
11 Information parameters select. (error monitor, condensed, topic, prime word flagging, constant input)
12 Lock in selected data.
13 Screen off.

Accessible Files List (partial)
Village map
Village underground
Operations: previous / current / future
Village personnel
Project Prisoner
'The Village Files'
Nomenclature list
Special documents
Prisoner files and dossiers
   - progress reports
   - information
   - surveillance photographs and video tapes
Village Mandate
Illuminati files
Village expansion plans
Satellite image photographs
Resuscitation procedures

Alerts
Yellow   • heightened awareness and vigilance.
Orange • Rover activation.
Red   • for use in Situation FallOut.

Video Transmissions
Transmissions of video signals from cameras in the field to receivers in the control room is by way of microwave frequencies. The field cameras (standard or concealed) contain internal or external microwave transmitters that send the video information in a condensed form from the MASER (Microwave Amplification by Stimulated Emission of Radiation) unit in the direction of the control room through a narrow beam. The SeeSaw in the control room rotates 360°, and tilts 20° above the horizontal to allow the receivers on each end, to pass by the signals that are sent. Field cameras are located all around the grounds of the Village, and each sends a constant microwave beam directly toward the control room. The senior observers see the image sent to them for 1.2 seconds before a new signal from a different camera is received. A signal that may be missed on one pass will be received by the observer on the opposite end of the SeeSaw as it turns.

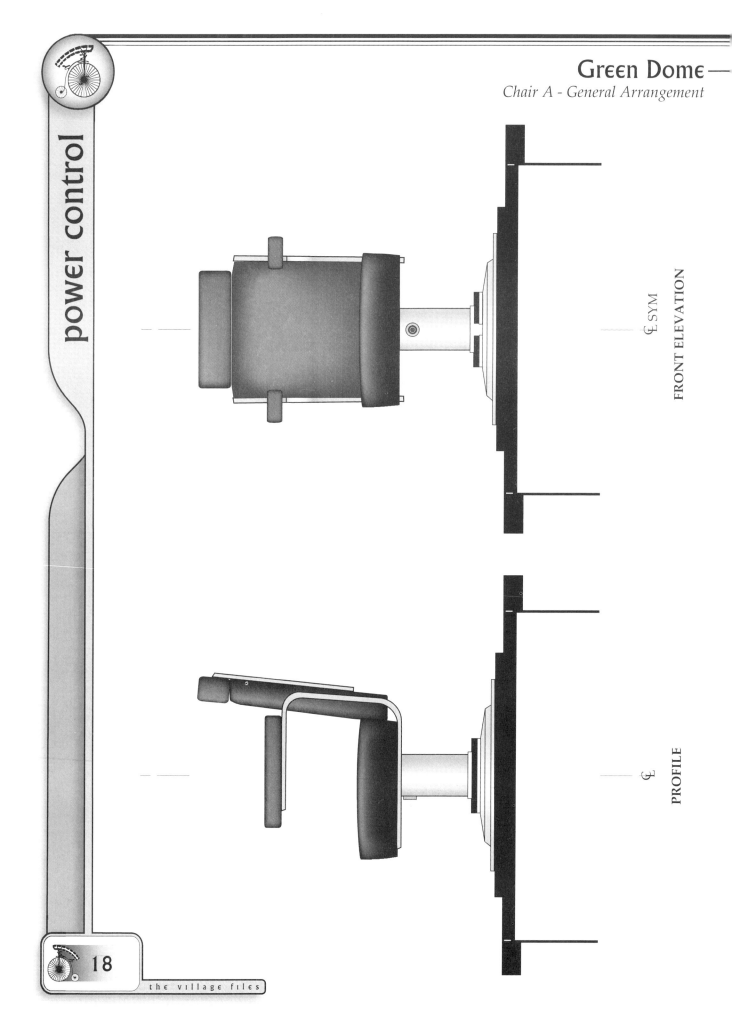

$\mathcal{C}$ SYM

FRONT ELEVATION

$\mathcal{C}$

PROFILE

Green Dome
Chair B - General Arrangement

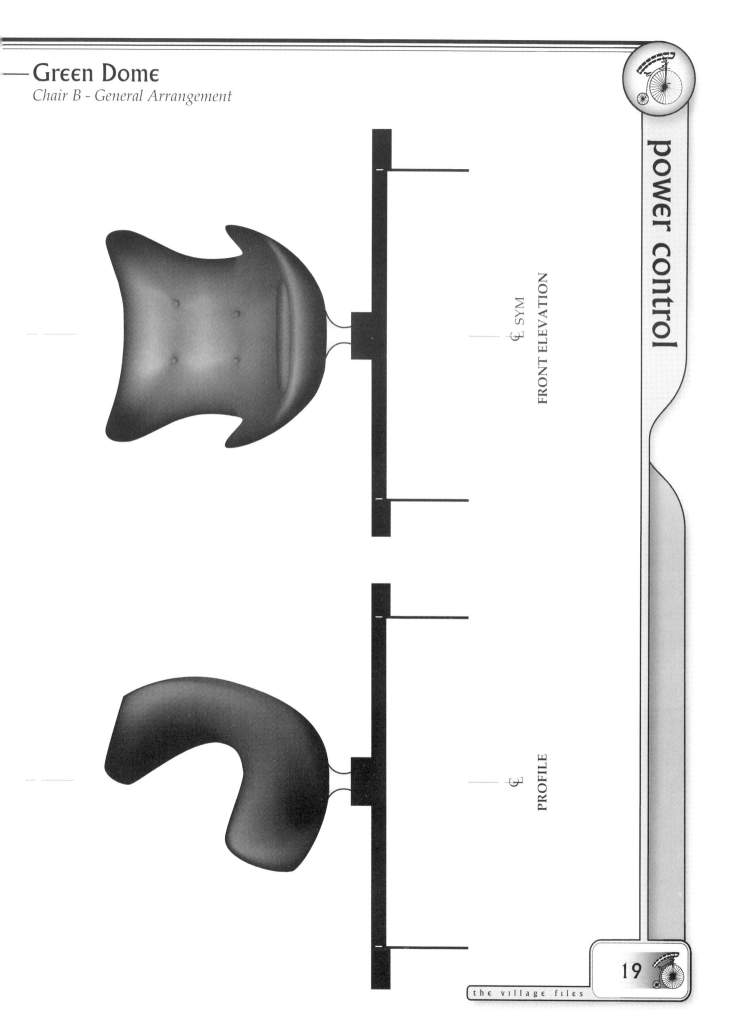

$\mathrm{C\!\!\!L}$ SYM

FRONT ELEVATION

$\mathrm{C\!\!\!L}$

PROFILE

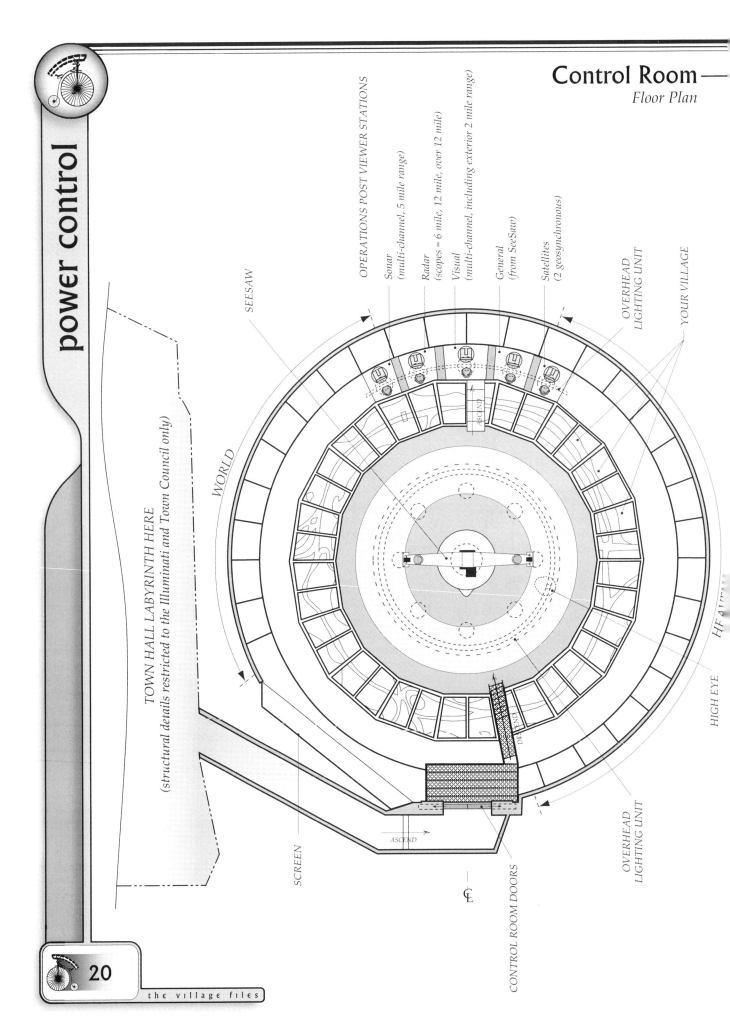

Control Room—
Floor Plan

OPERATIONS POST VIEWER STATIONS

Sonar
(multi-channel, 5 mile range)

Radar
(scopes = 6 mile, 12 mile, over 12 mile)

Visual
(multi-channel, including exterior 2 mile range)

General
(from SeeSaw)

Satellites
(2 geosynchronous)

OVERHEAD
LIGHTING UNIT

YOUR VILLAGE

SEESAW

ASCEND

WORLD

DESCEND

HIGH EYE

SCREEN

ASCEND

C
L

CONTROL ROOM DOORS

OVERHEAD
LIGHTING UNIT

TOWN HALL LABYRINTH HERE
(structural details restricted to the Illuminati and Town Council only)

—Control Room
SeeSaw - Profile Arrangement

SEESAW VIEWER

SENIOR OBSERVER POSTS

FULCRUM

20°

TELEPHONE RECEIVER
PLACEMENT

℄ SYM

ROTATION MACHINERY

21

power control

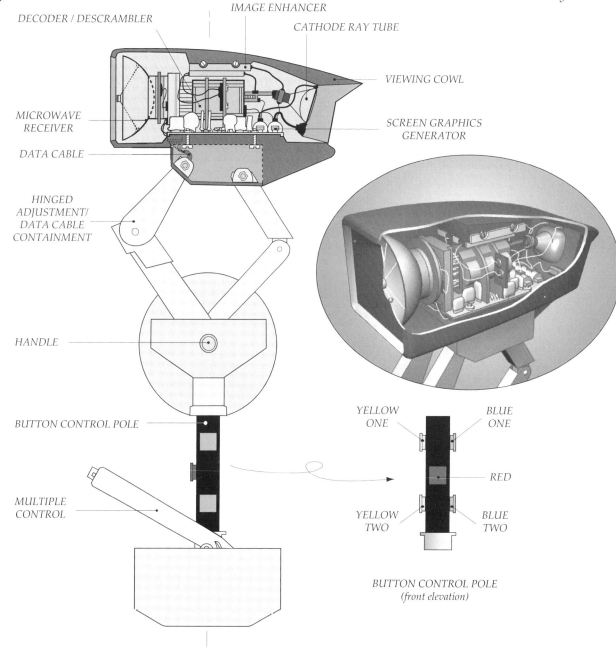

DECODER / DESCRAMBLER

IMAGE ENHANCER

CATHODE RAY TUBE

VIEWING COWL

MICROWAVE RECEIVER

SCREEN GRAPHICS GENERATOR

DATA CABLE

HINGED ADJUSTMENT/ DATA CABLE CONTAINMENT

HANDLE

BUTTON CONTROL POLE

MULTIPLE CONTROL

YELLOW ONE

BLUE ONE

RED

YELLOW TWO

BLUE TWO

BUTTON CONTROL POLE
(front elevation)

CONTROL POLE BUTTONS

RED
- image shunt
- shunts image to post observer
for further scrutiny.

BLUE ONE
- flag image to review on next pass.

BLUE TWO
- call up previously flagged image.

YELLOW ONE
- store image on screen to study
more accurately.

YELLOW TWO
- release previously stored image
to continue accepting images
from microwave receiver.

—Control Room
Operations Post Viewer - General Arrangement

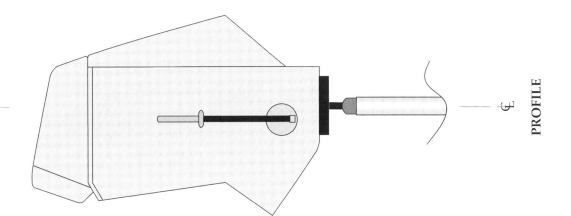

VIEWING COWL

CHANNEL SELECTOR

CHANNEL DATA DISPLAY

PARAMETERS DISPLAY

℄ SYM

FRONT ELEVATION

℄

PROFILE

power control

VIDEO SAFE AREA

TIME / DATE STAMP

ALERT STATUS LIGHT
(yellow / orange / red)

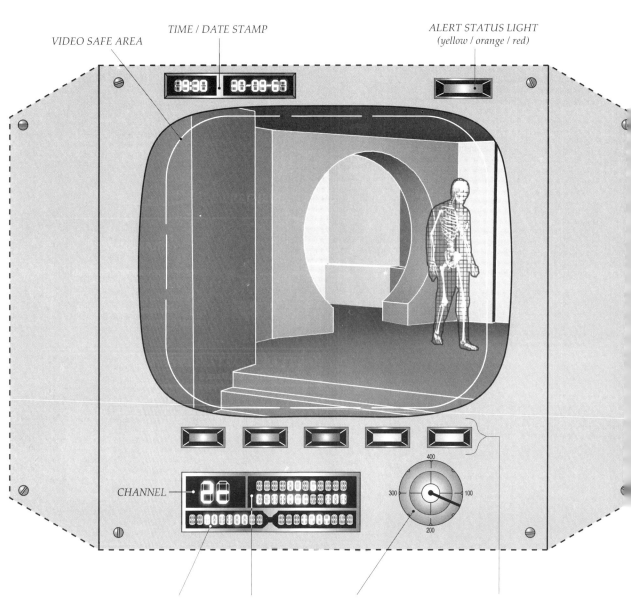

CHANNEL

VIEWING MODES
(Vector Enhancement)
(Infrared)
(X-ray)
(Visible Light)
(Ultraviolet)
(Motionmap Examine)

LOCATION

CONTROLLER
DIRECTION
(gradients X 400)
*(degrees X 360 also
available)*

BUTTON SELECT LIGHTS
- *blue two*
- *blue one*
- *shunt*
- *yellow one*
- *yellow two*

Rover *(Reactive Orange-alert Vigilant EnforceR)*
General Arrangement

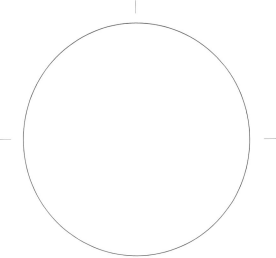

FRONT ELEVATION

PROFILE

TOP PLAN

₵L

- TOWING MODE -

Double appendages are
deployed to tow a load.
Maximum Load: 20 stone
Subject's arms must be
outstretched if over 10 stone.

(direction of movement)

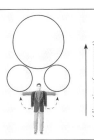

ROVER ATTACK PATTERN
(at maximum gallop)

ARCED ATTACK VECTORS ($\gamma\theta$)

MAXIMUM OPTIONAL
TANGENT ANGLE
FOR MOTION
REDIRECTION
DECISION

60°

13 ft

6.2 ft

PRISONER

STATISTICS

Maximum Expansion Diameter: *8 ft.*
(3 foot appendages available in towing mode).
Maximum Speed: *12 mph.*
Control Source: *Autonomous Operation Mechanism*
Patrol Locales: *All horizontal and vertical via van der Waals' force.*
Sensory Apparatus: *Shape and movement discrimination with visible light,*
infrared wavelength, and optical recognition capabilities.
External Structure: *Malleable Pseudo-Geodesic Euclidian Sphere*
utilising homopolymer / copolymer blends.
Internal Mechanisms: *That Would Be Telling.*

SUBDUING TECHNIQUE

NOTE: *Some cottages contain Rover friendly "Ease of Entry"
doorways, shaped to fit Rover. The cottage of Number 6 contains
one of these entry ways.*

power control

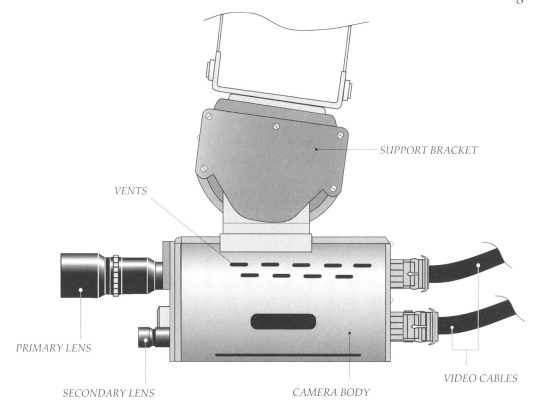

SUPPORT BRACKET

VENTS

PRIMARY LENS

SECONDARY LENS

CAMERA BODY

VIDEO CABLES

PROFILE

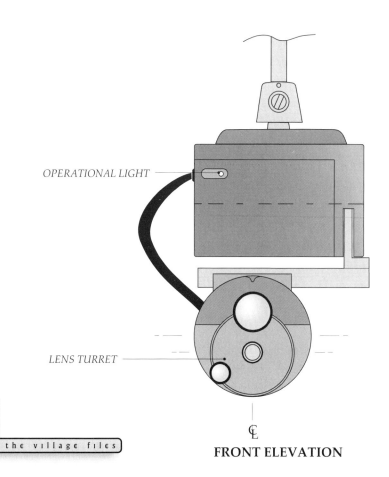

OPERATIONAL LIGHT

LENS TURRET

℄

FRONT ELEVATION

—Concealed Camera
Cutaway View

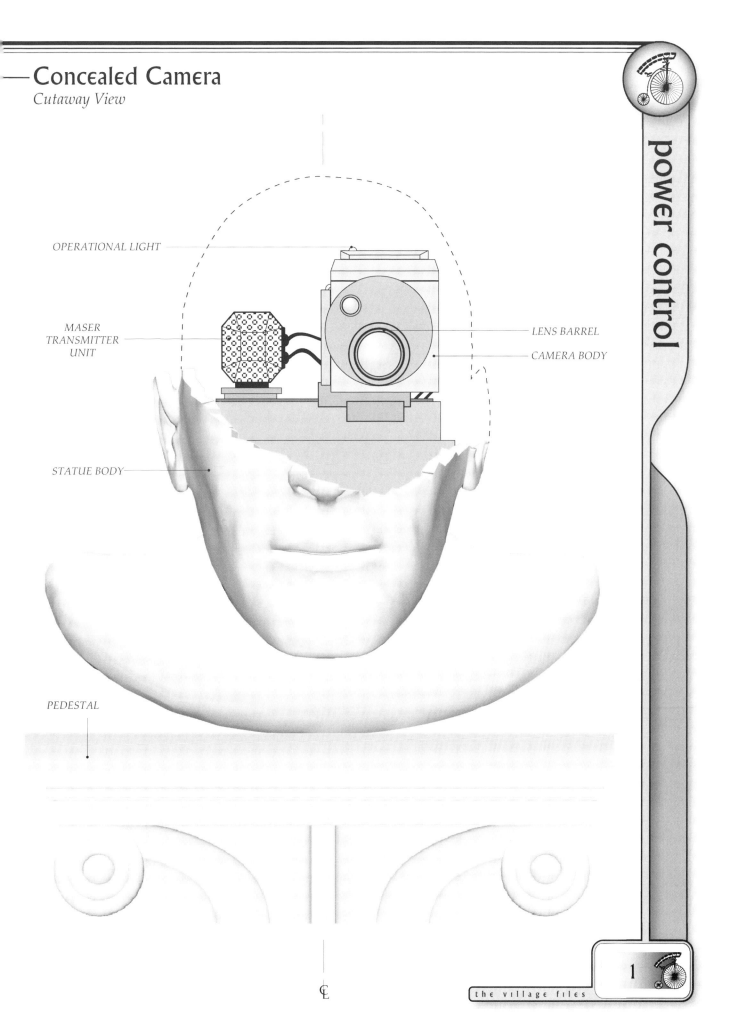

OPERATIONAL LIGHT

MASER
TRANSMITTER
UNIT

LENS BARREL

CAMERA BODY

STATUE BODY

PEDESTAL

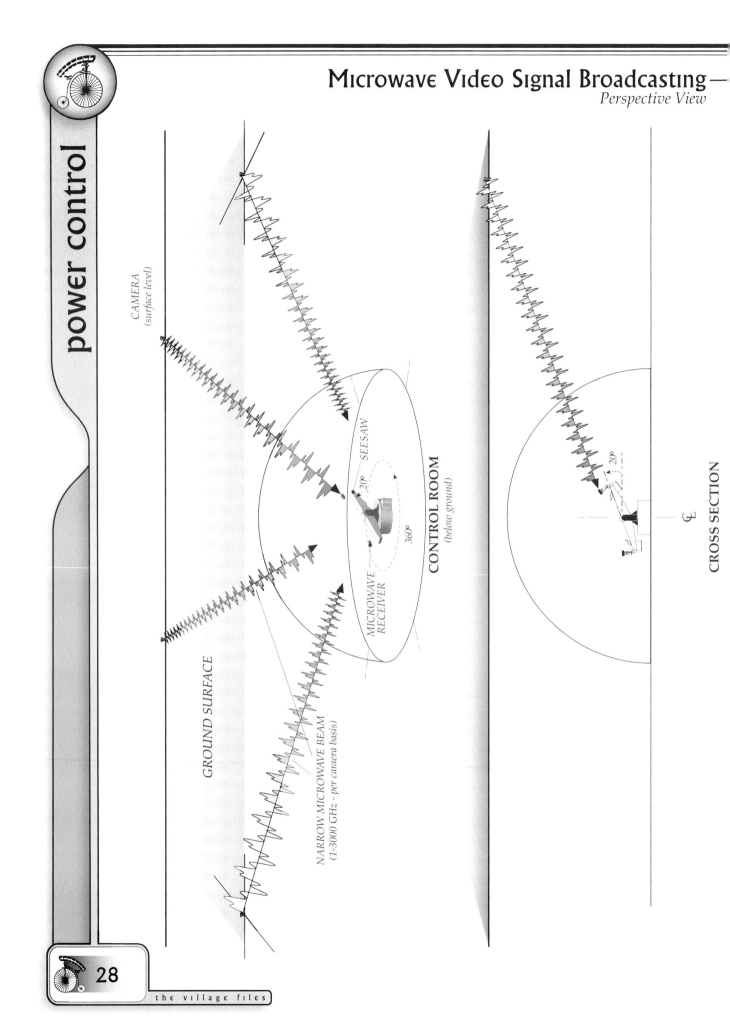

power control

CAMERA
(surface level)

GROUND SURFACE

NARROW MICROWAVE BEAM
(1-3000 GHz – per camera basis)

SEESAW

20°

360°

MICROWAVE
RECEIVER

CONTROL ROOM
(below ground)

20°

℄

CROSS SECTION

habitation

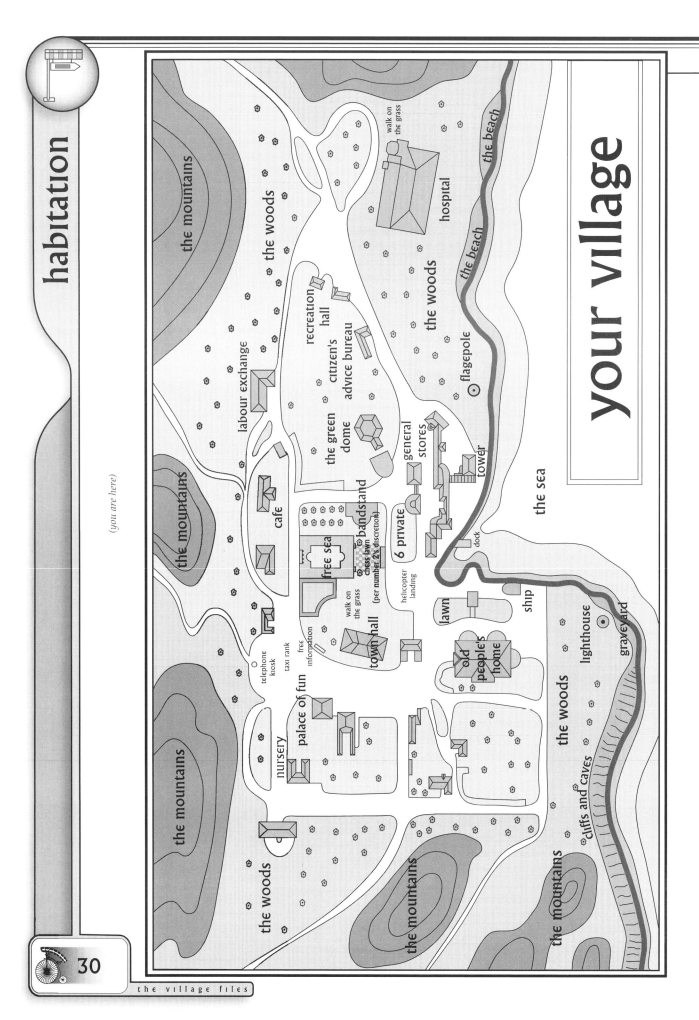

(you are here)

the mountains

the mountains

the mountains

the woods

the woods

the woods

the woods

the woods

the mountains

the mountains

the mountains

the woods

walk on the grass

hospital

the beach

the beach

recreation hall

citizen's advice bureau

labour exchange

flagepole

the green dome

general stores

tower

cafe

bandstand

free sea

chess lawn
(per number 2's discretion)

6 private

the sea

helicopter landing

dock

ship

lawn

walk on the grass

town hall

free information

taxi rank

telephone kiosk

palace of fun

nursery

old people's home

lighthouse

graveyard

cliffs and caves

your village

—Free Information
General Arrangement

FREE INFORMATION

SELECT YOUR DESTINATION AND PRESS THE CORRESPONDING BUTTON

(your village)

your village

PUSH AND FIND OUT

28 fun palace
36 hospital
14 shop
9 taxi rank
10 council
8 bandstand
4 exchange
1 town hall
5 **old people**
3 old home
18 ship

READY FOR OPERATION · MACHINE IN OPERATION · END OF OPERATION

FRONT ELEVATION

PROFILE

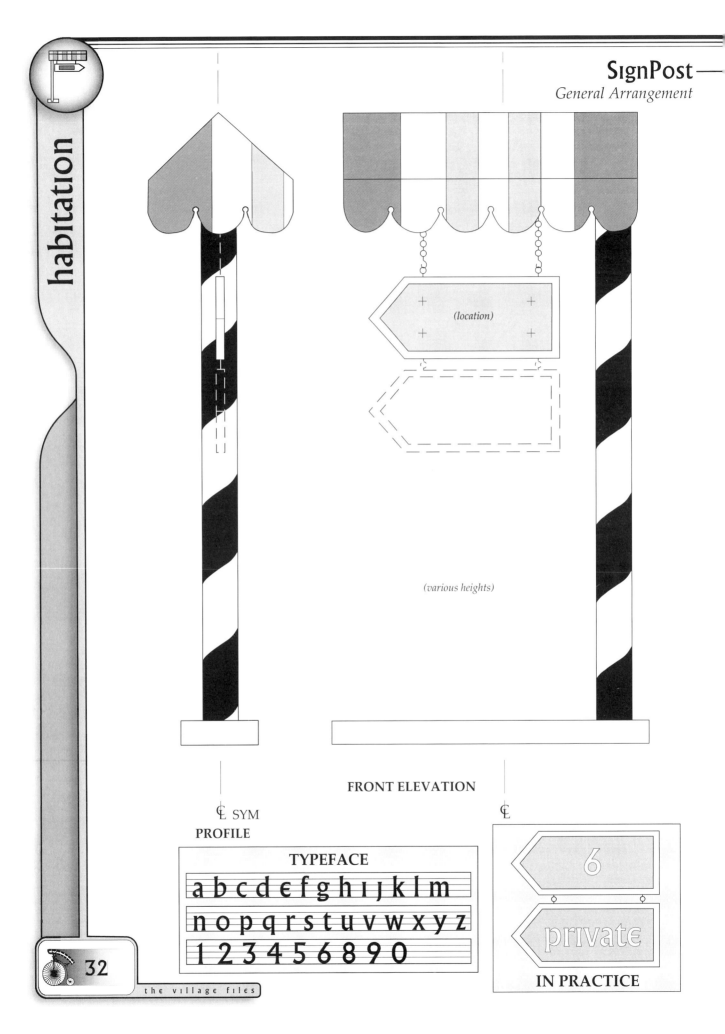

habitation

(location)

(various heights)

FRONT ELEVATION

Ȼ SYM
PROFILE

Ȼ

TYPEFACE

abcdefghijklm

nopqrstuvwxyz

1234568 90

6

private

IN PRACTICE

SpeakerPole
General Arrangement

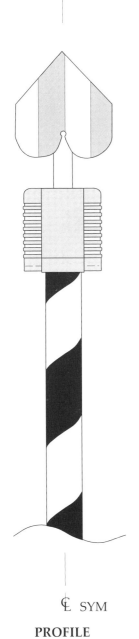

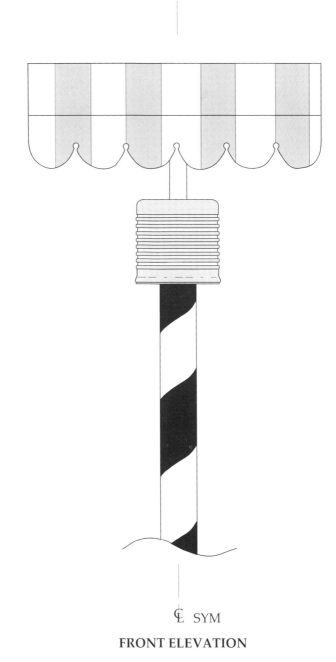

℄ SYM

PROFILE

℄ SYM

FRONT ELEVATION

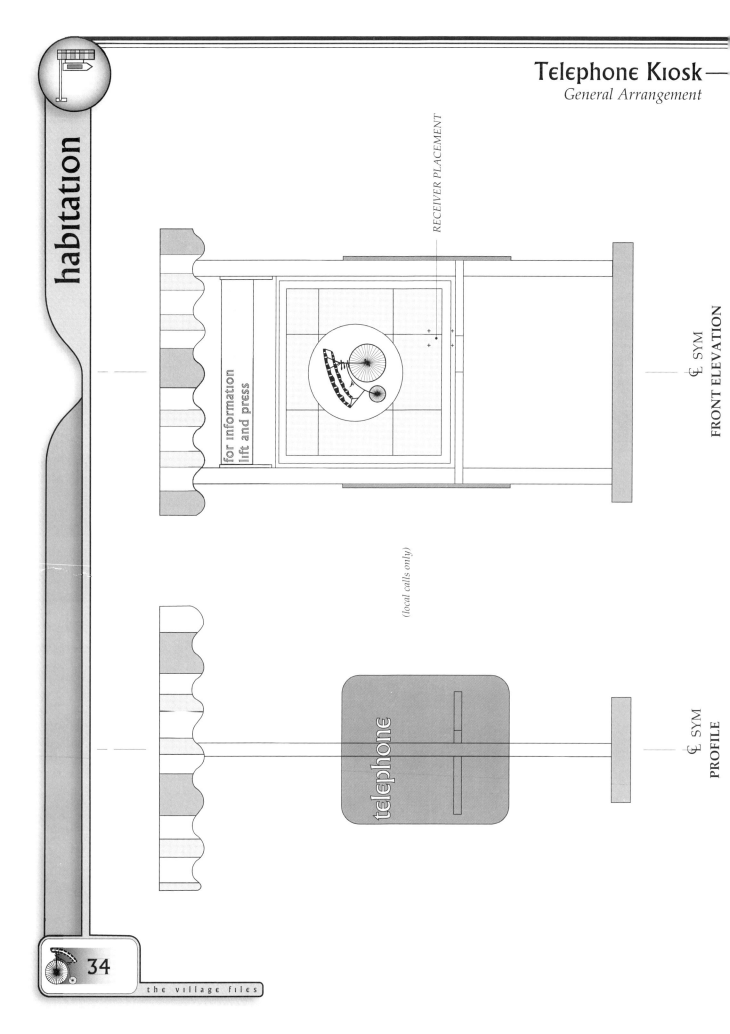

Telephone Kiosk—
General Arrangement

RECEIVER PLACEMENT

for information
lift and press

℄ SYM
FRONT ELEVATION

(local calls only)

telephone

℄ SYM
PROFILE

Telephone Receiver
General Arrangement

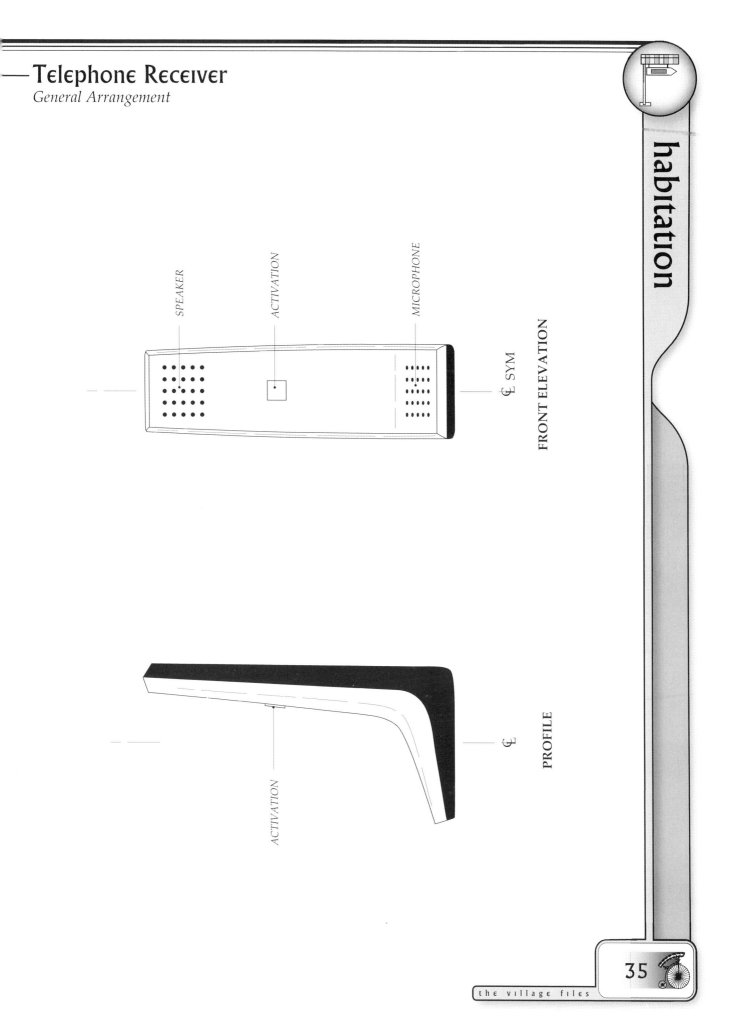

SPEAKER

ACTIVATION

MICROPHONE

℄ SYM

FRONT ELEVATION

ACTIVATION

℄

PROFILE

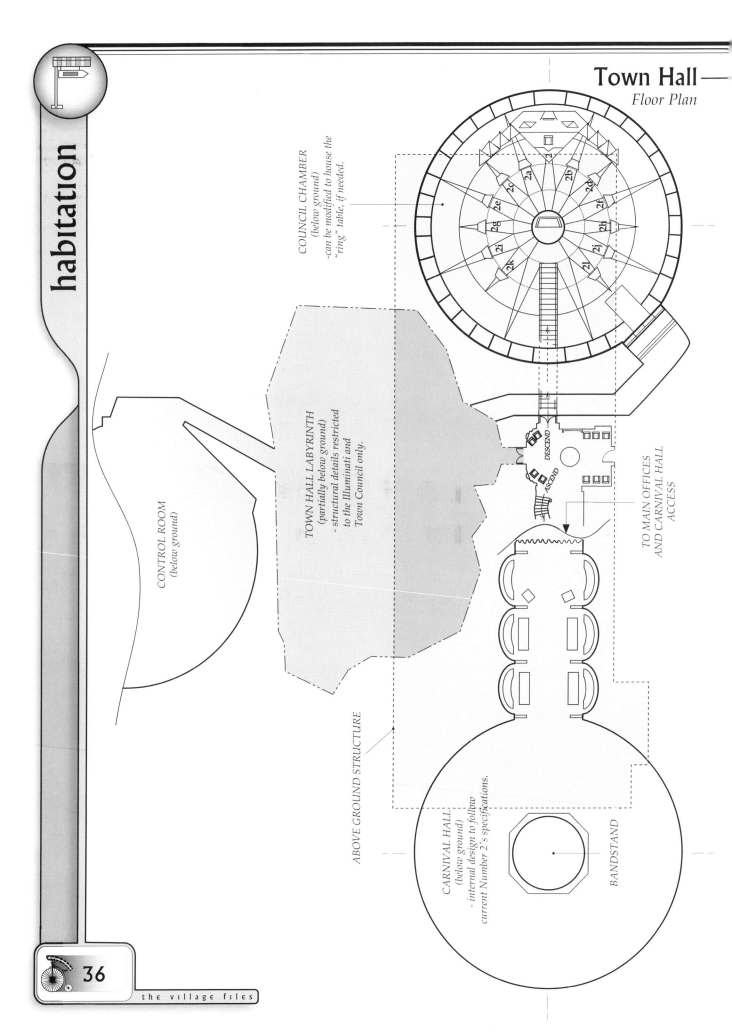

COUNCIL CHAMBER
(below ground)
-can be modified to house the
"ring" table, if needed.

2a 2b 2c 2d 2e 2f 2g 2h 2i 2j 2k 2l

DESCEND

ASCEND

TOWN HALL LABYRINTH
(partially below ground)
-structural details restricted
to the Illuminati and
Town Council only.

CONTROL ROOM
(below ground)

ABOVE GROUND STRUCTURE

TO MAIN OFFICES
AND CARNIVAL HALL
ACCESS

CARNIVAL HALL
(below ground)
- internal design to follow
current Number 2's specifications.

BANDSTAND

Labour Exchange
Floor Plan

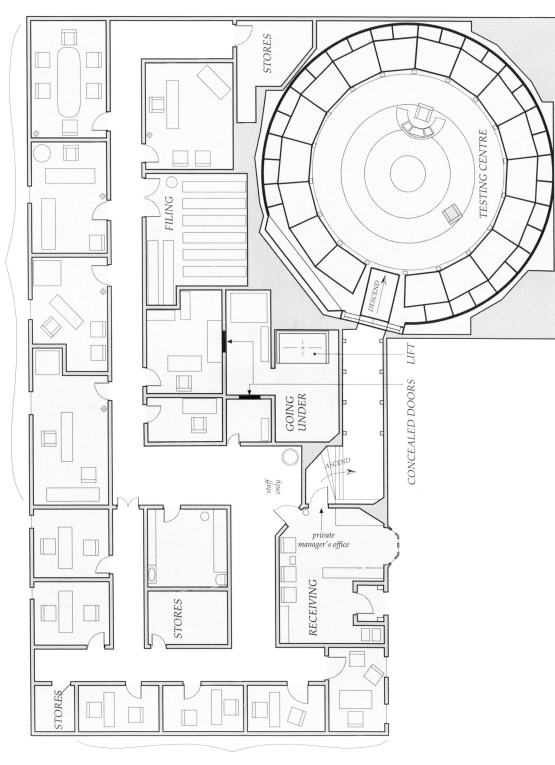

STORES

ADMINISTERING

FILING

STORES

TESTING CENTRE

DESCEND

GOING UNDER

LIFT

CONCEALED DOORS

ASCEND

staff only

private manager's office

RECEIVING

STORES

CAREER INTERROGATING

habitation

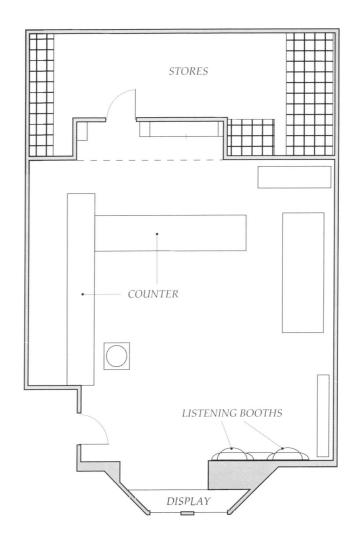

STORES

COUNTER

LISTENING BOOTHS

DISPLAY

—Good Food
Label Detail

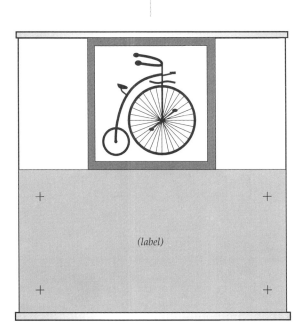

(label)

℄ SYM   ℄ SYM

(shown actual size)

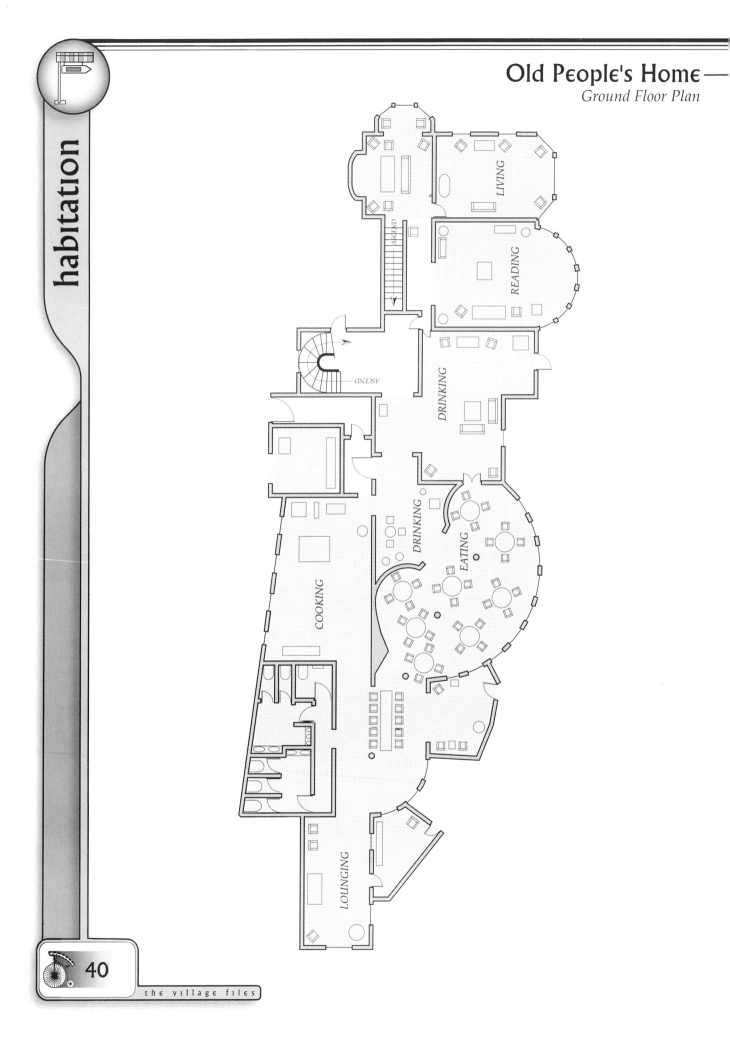

Old People's Home—
Ground Floor Plan

habitation

LIVING

READING

ASCEND

DRINKING

ASCEND

DRINKING

EATING

COOKING

LOUNGING

Old People's Home
1st / 2nd Floor Plans

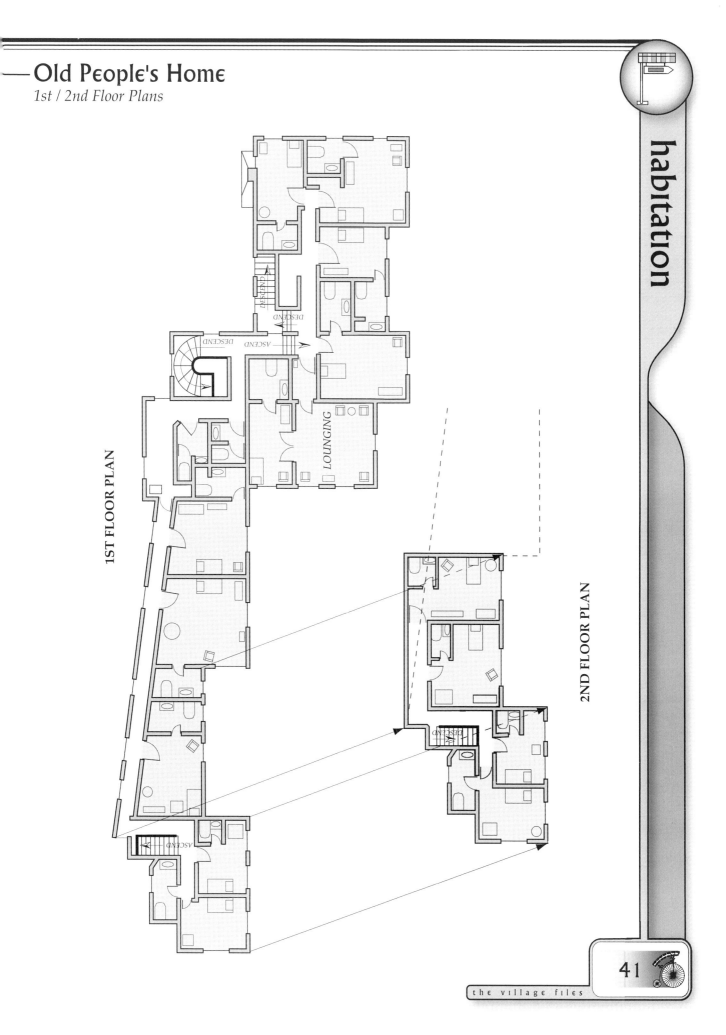

1ST FLOOR PLAN

LOUNGING

2ND FLOOR PLAN

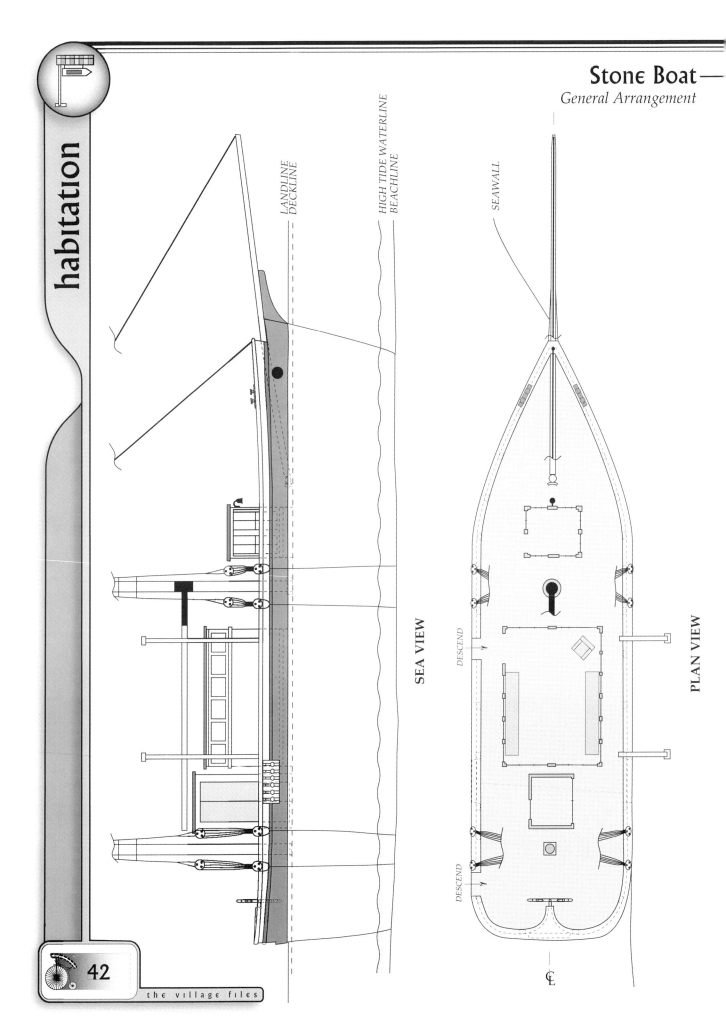

Stone Boat—
General Arrangement

LANDLINE
DECKLINE

HIGH TIDE WATERLINE
BEACHLINE

SEAWALL

SEA VIEW

PLAN VIEW

DESCEND

DESCEND

C̶L

going under

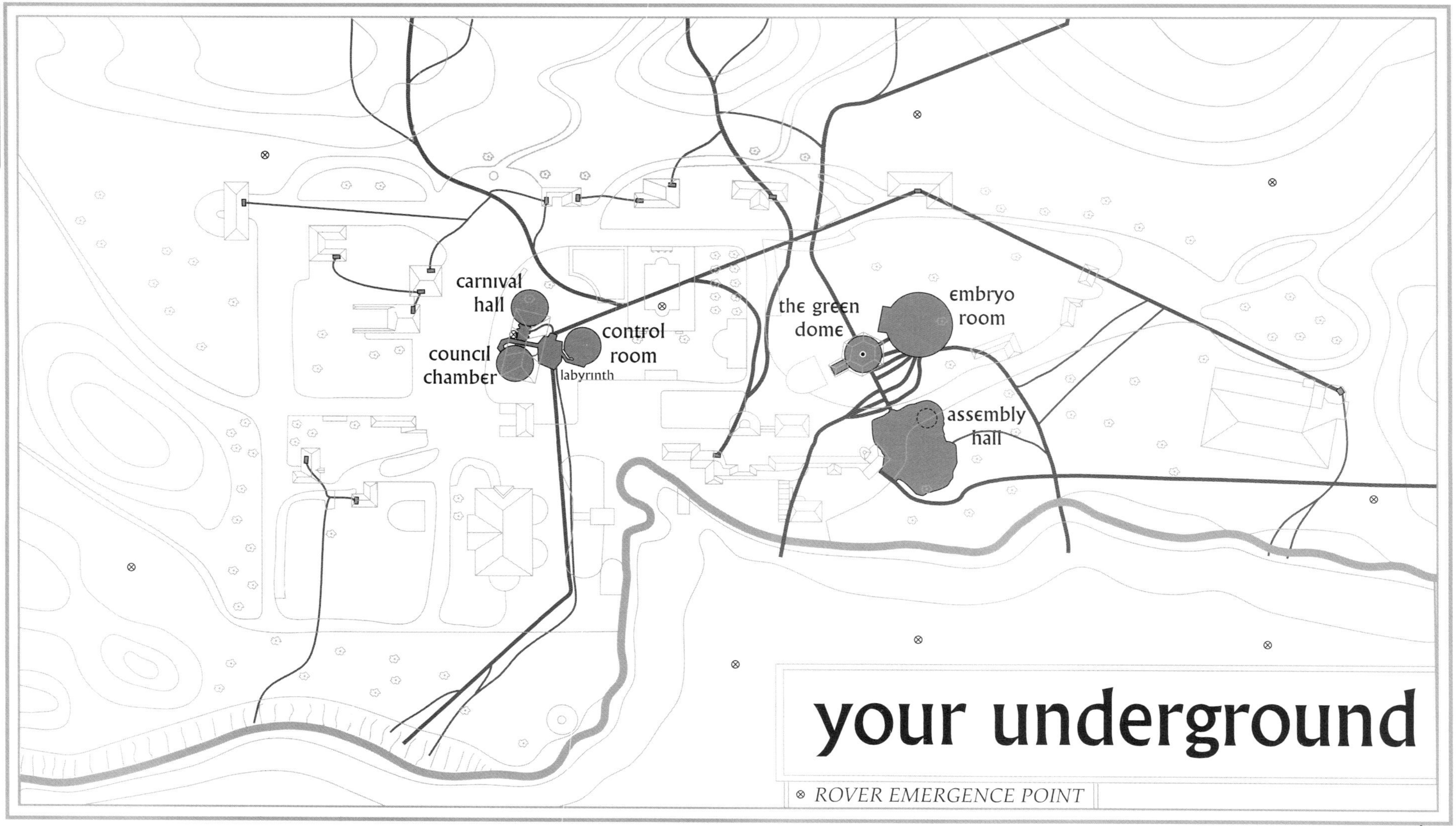

your underground

⊗ *ROVER EMERGENCE POINT*

embryo room

assembly hall

the green dome

control room

labyrinth

carnival hall

council chamber

—Underground
Cross-Section View

GREEN DOME

EMBRYO ROOM
(encased in steel)

CLOAK ROOM

(floor plan)

**CROSS SECTION THROUGH
DESCENDING SHAFT FROM GREEN DOME**

(assembly hall here)

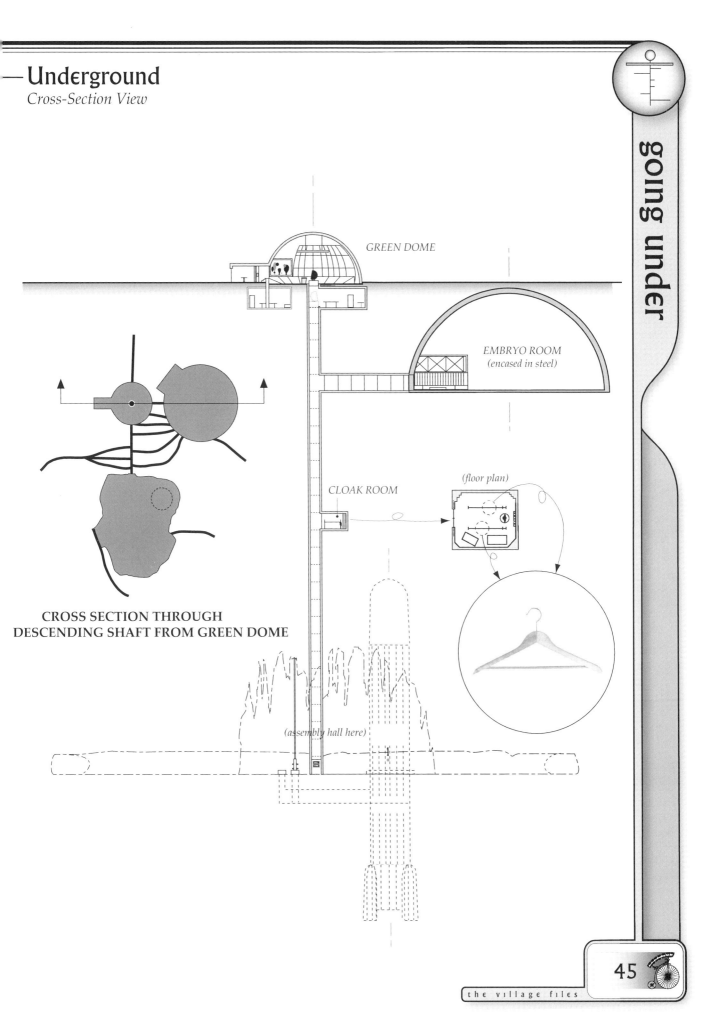

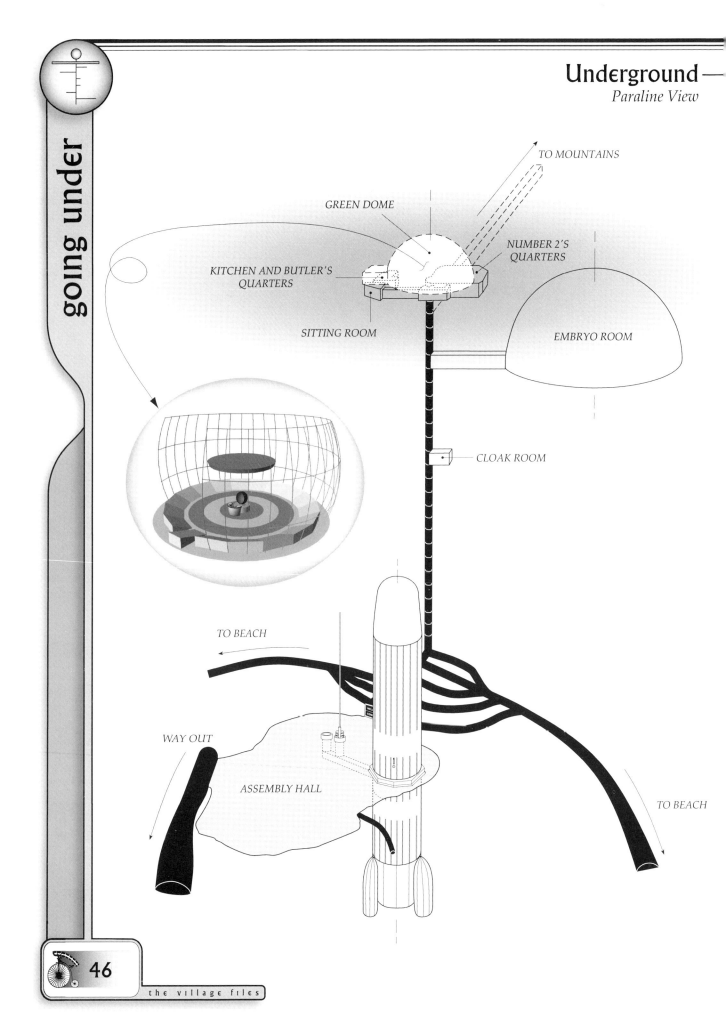

TO MOUNTAINS

GREEN DOME

NUMBER 2'S QUARTERS

KITCHEN AND BUTLER'S QUARTERS

SITTING ROOM

EMBRYO ROOM

CLOAK ROOM

TO BEACH

WAY OUT

ASSEMBLY HALL

TO BEACH

Assembly Hall
Floor Plan

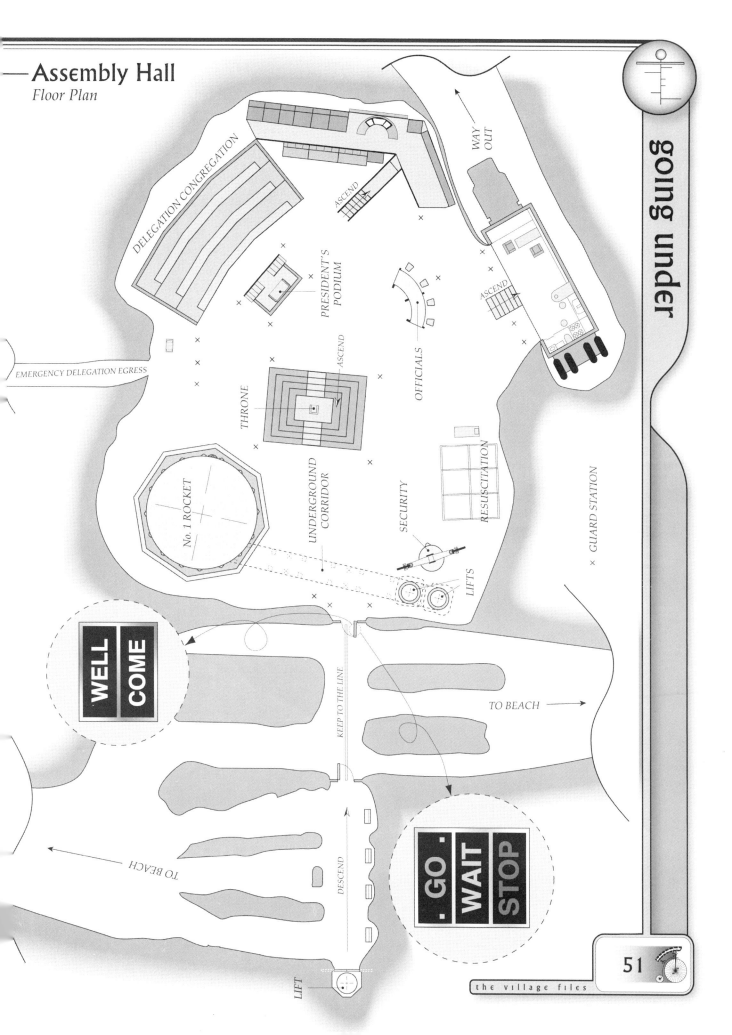

DELEGATION CONGREGATION

ASCEND

WAY OUT

PRESIDENT'S PODIUM

ASCEND

EMERGENCY DELEGATION EGRESS

OFFICIALS

THRONE

ASCEND

UNDERGROUND CORRIDOR

SECURITY

RESUSCITATION

No. 1 ROCKET

GUARD STATION

LIFTS

WELL COME

KEEP TO THE LINE

TO BEACH

TO BEACH

DESCEND

GO . WAIT STOP

LIFT

going under

ACCOMMODATION
NUTRITION
BOARD
ADMINISTRATION
PRAGMATISTS
ARCHANGELS
GOVERN
OBSERVERS
HEALTH

SECURITY
REHABILITATION
EDUCATION
OLD FOLK
UNMUTUALS
UNITARIANS
COMMITTEE
TRANSPORTATION

IDENTIFICATION
DEFECTORS
THERAPY
REACTIONISTS
NATIONALISTS
ENTERTAINMENT
RECREATION
ACTIVISTS
ANARCHISTS
YOUNGSTERS
PACIFISTS
WELFARE

Assembly Hall
Rocket Room - Underground Level Floor Plan

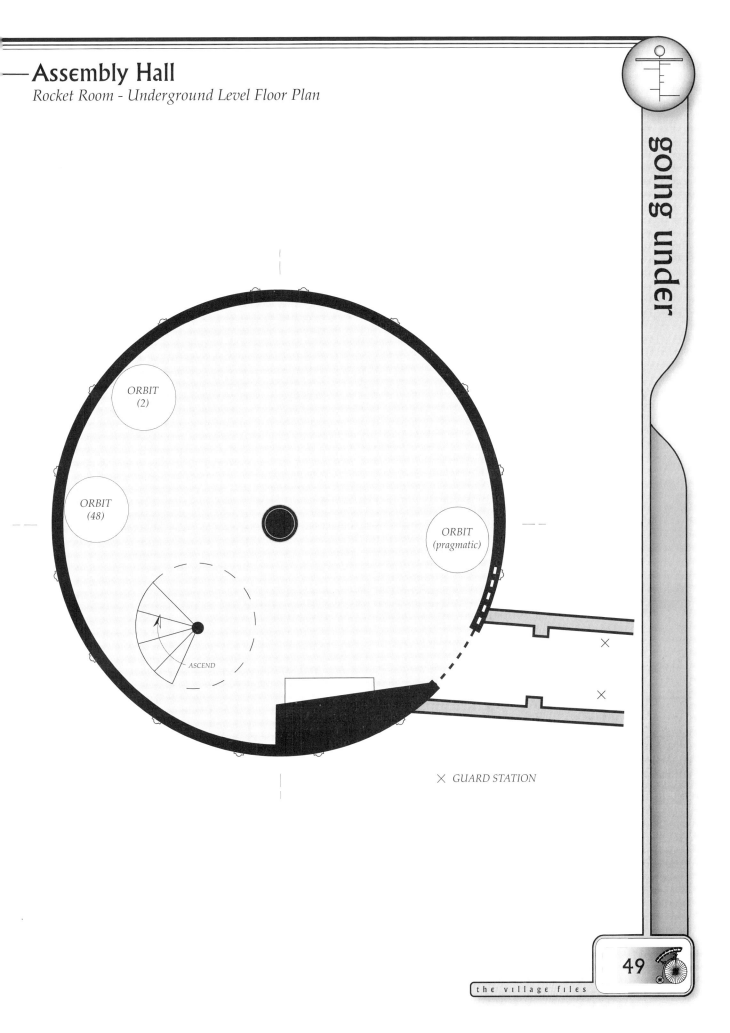

ORBIT
(2)

ORBIT
(48)

ORBIT
(pragmatic)

ASCEND

✕ *GUARD STATION*

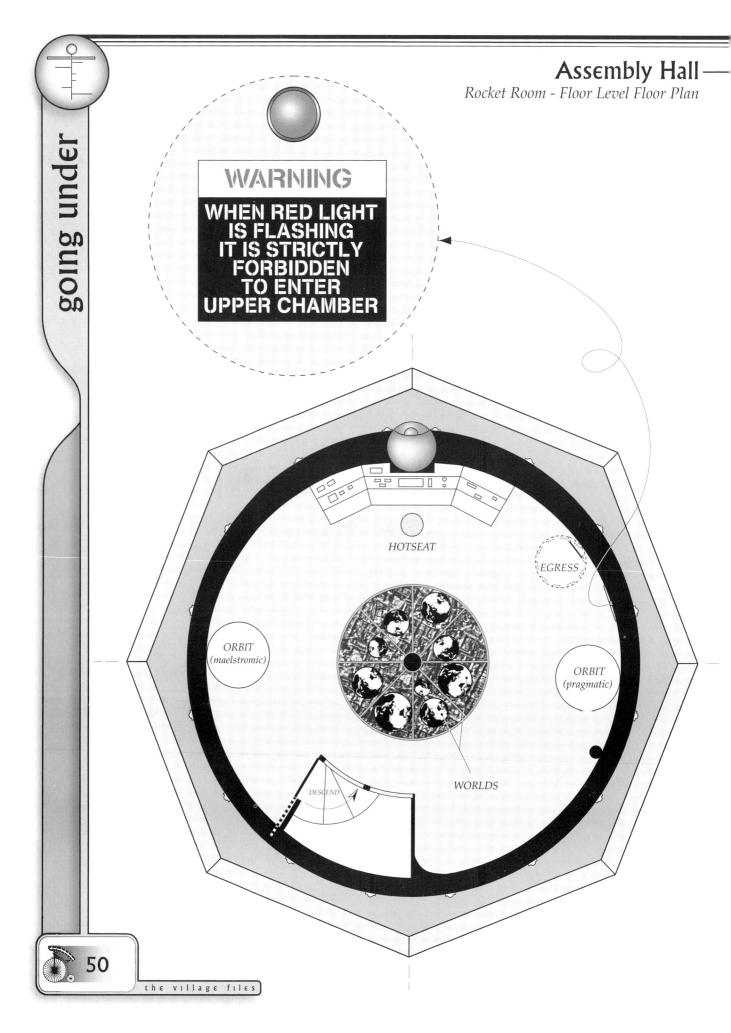

going under

WARNING
WHEN RED LIGHT IS FLASHING IT IS STRICTLY FORBIDDEN TO ENTER UPPER CHAMBER

HOTSEAT

EGRESS

ORBIT
(maelstromic)

ORBIT
(pragmatic)

WORLDS

DESCEND

SCIENCES

Group Therapy
This type of behavioural therapy counteracts obsessional guilt complexes producing neurosis.

Aversion Therapy
In this type of behaviour therapy, the 'id' is tapped, altered, and controlled to have an aversion to many different possible images, including Rover, Number 2, and the idea of escape.

Truth Test
The truth test is performed in the testing centre of the Labour Exchange. It is used to reach beyond the subject's normal mental resistance to interrogation, and get to the truth. On the schematic, the ball is the lie indicator, and moves when the subject's thoughts are deceptive. The cube is the truth indicator, and has motion when the subject's thoughts are truthful.

Multi-Phasic Personality Test
This test experiments in altering the subject's base **personality using var**ying phasic bands of waves (å waves, ß waves, etc.).

Thematic Apperception Test
Based in cognitive neuroscience. How the subject perceives reality and processes sensory input from the outside world is tested. These can be changed to the Illuminati's parameters.

Sonic Surgery
The uses of sonic surgery are varied. A lobotomy as a step in Instant Social Conversion being one example. The main component is a unit containing a quartz crystal activated by a variable electromagnetic field from high voltage condensers. The crystal emits ultra-sonic sound waves which are bounced off of a parabolic reflector. The focal point of the reflector can be seen by the use of light waves. The prime concern is to locate the link point of the subject's frontal lobes. Application of a gel-based lanolin barrier to the skin is used to minimise external cell breakdown and scarring. At the discretion of the attending doctor, a relaxant can be injected to reduce muscular tension. The final step is to step up the voltage until the ultra-sonic bombardment causes permanent dislocation. (see: Operation Mind Change -MINDCH-).

Shock Treatment
Shock treatment is used in aversion therapy, and the multi-phasic personality test. It can even be used to simply change the subject's voluntary and involuntary reflexes. Combining it with the multi-phasic personality test, changing reflexes is possible (see: Operation Schizoid -SCHIZ-). Multi-model therapy (cognitive-behavioural) can be combined with shock treatment for quicker results. When utilising shock treatment, the patient will be doing fine.

Drugs
By using drugs like serotonin (5-hydroxytryptamine) and various super-strength meprobomates a prisoner can be controlled. After infusing a certain meprobomate into a subject, the meprobomate will remain dormant until triggered by the nervous system. It releases itself to the desired quantity to produce instant tranquility or temporary oblivion. Of course a side effect of such a drug is the contraction of the subject's pupils and lack of short term memory. (see: Operation Funeral -FUN-) Other drugs in use in the Village may be electrochemical in nature and are used to control and / or paralyse a prisoner's neural architecture. These include monoxynulleoallanine, MDMA, and ketamine hydrochloride.

Degree Absolute
This procedure has operating parameters known only to Number 2, and the Illuminati.

Resuscitation
Resuscitation is used only during Plan Pantheon. It is used to repair pernicious problems resulting from Degree Absolute.

Clones
MOST SECRET

Forcefields
Forcefields are in operation at the entrance of the Town Hall, and at the entrance to the Town Hall Labyrinth. They operate on a computer-controlled optical recognition programme.

Pulsator
The pulsator can be used simply to deepen the subject's sleep and keep him or her pacified, or to go as far as changing the subject's profundity by utilising the nerve cell manipulating actuator. A pulsator assembly is located in every prisoner's cottage.

Hospital

Ground Floor Plan

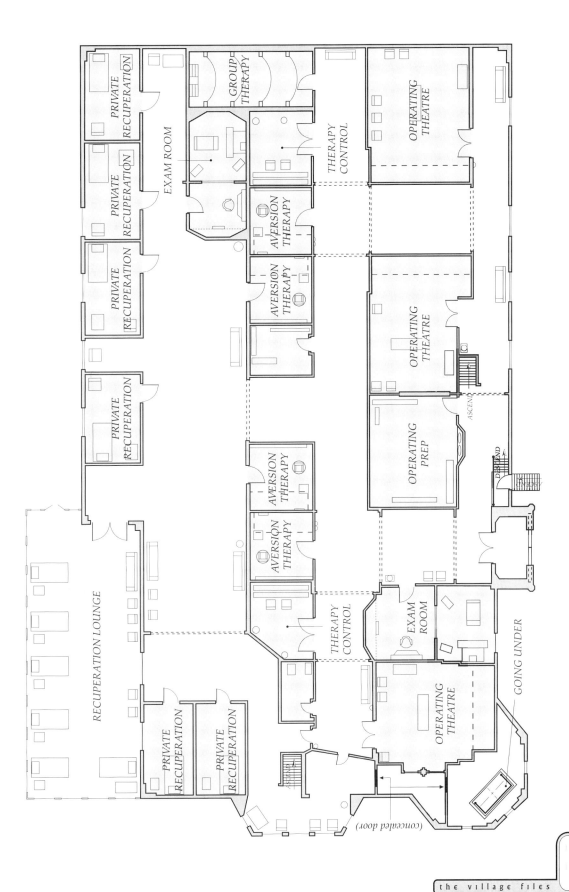

SCIENCES

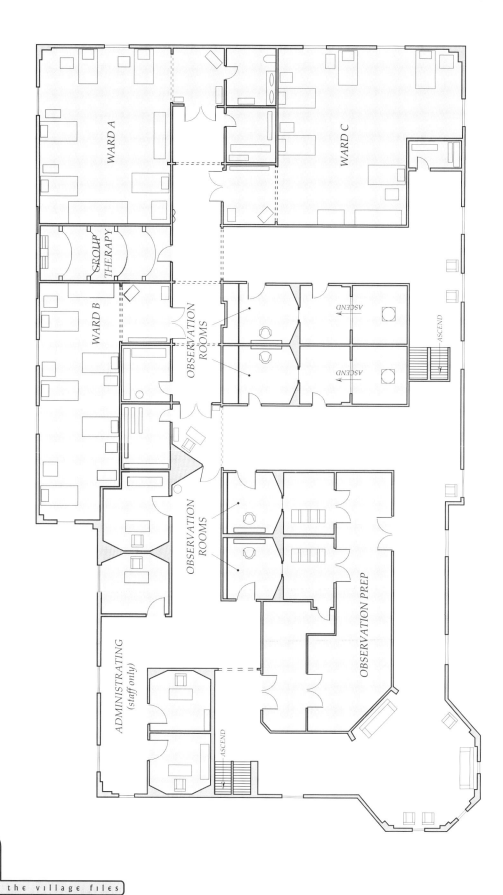

WARD A

WARD C

GROUP
THERAPY

WARD B

OBSERVATION
ROOMS

ASCEND

ASCEND

ASCEND

OBSERVATION
ROOMS

OBSERVATION PREP

ADMINISTRATING
(staff only)

ASCEND

Hospital

2nd Floor Plan

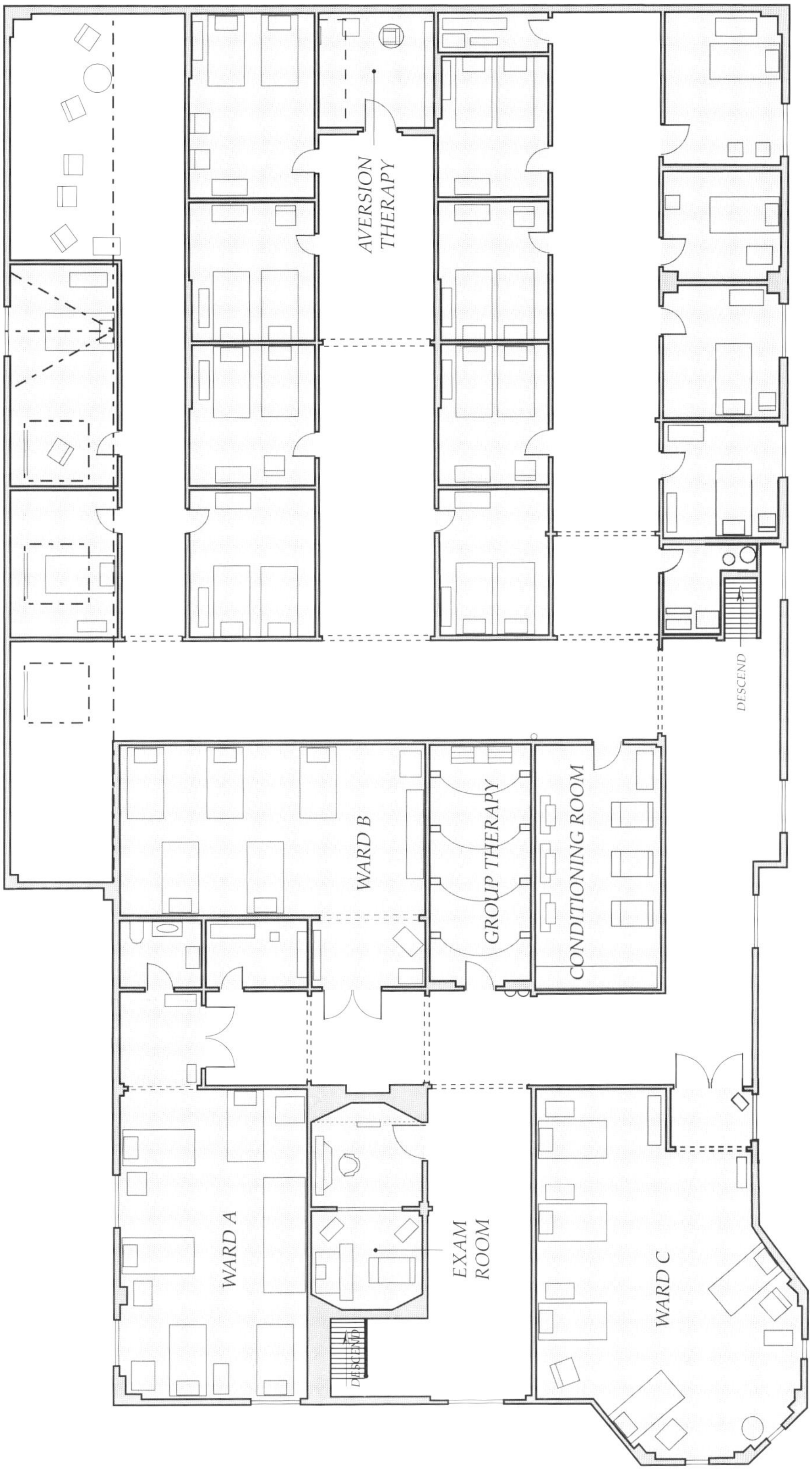
AVERSION THERAPY
WARD B
GROUP THERAPY
CONDITIONING ROOM
DESCEND
WARD A
EXAM ROOM
WARD C
DESCEND

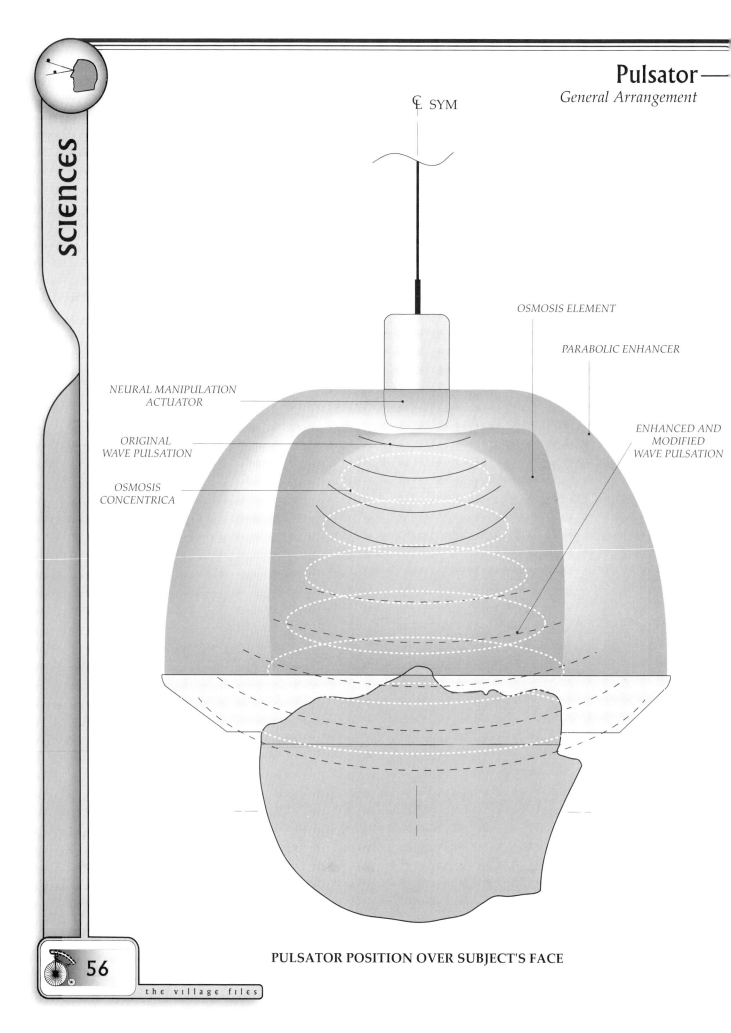

Pulsator—
General Arrangement

℄ SYM

OSMOSIS ELEMENT

PARABOLIC ENHANCER

NEURAL MANIPULATION
ACTUATOR

ENHANCED AND
MODIFIED
WAVE PULSATION

ORIGINAL
WAVE PULSATION

OSMOSIS
CONCENTRICA

PULSATOR POSITION OVER SUBJECT'S FACE

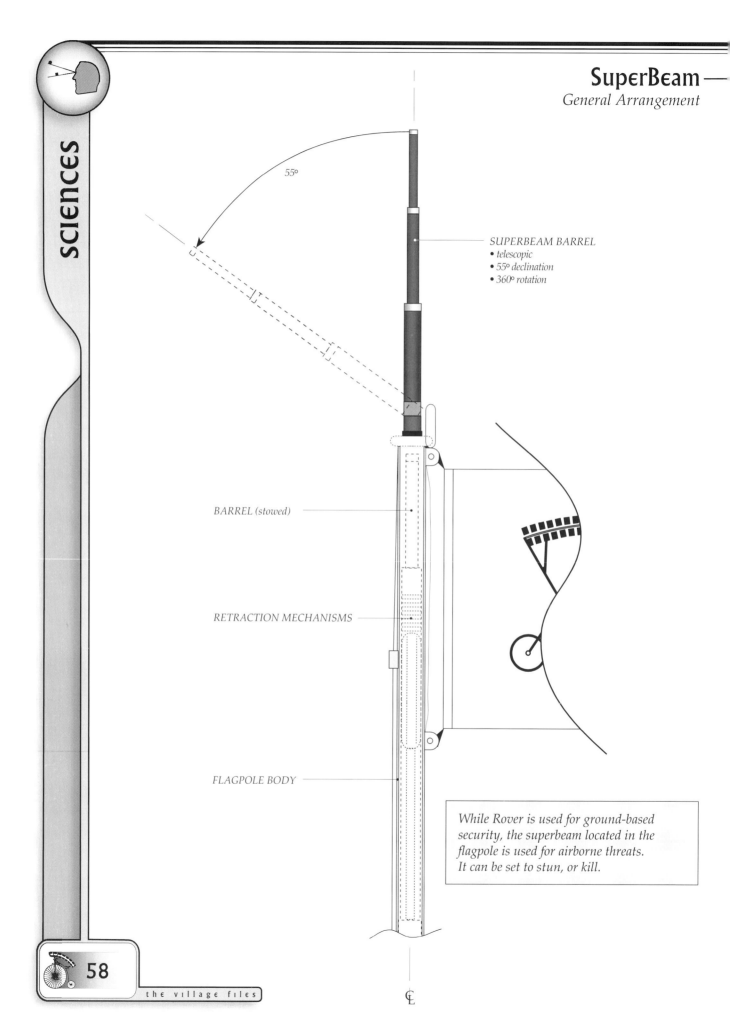

55°

SUPERBEAM BARREL
• telescopic
• 55° declination
• 360° rotation

BARREL (stowed)

RETRACTION MECHANISMS

FLAGPOLE BODY

While Rover is used for ground-based security, the superbeam located in the flagpole is used for airborne threats. It can be set to stun, or kill.

SCIENCES

illuminati

Illuminati

The Illuminati is the plenipotentiary force in the Village. The phalanx of 'Archangels' oversees operations and goings-on from their Pantheon. Their ultimate power is generally non-transferable, unless special conditions and situations arise. Inner workings of the Illuminati are nebulous at best.

The High Eye located in the Control Room is used to keep a plethora of ocular tabs on the activities of the Village. All plans, and operations must be cleared with the Illuminati before use, especially in the case of Number 6 (see: Project Prisoner -PRIS-). Entire details of the 'Gods', are classified beyond HUSH MOST SECRET. Classification of the level of classification of the Illuminati is: VERY SECRET.

— High Eye
General Arrangement

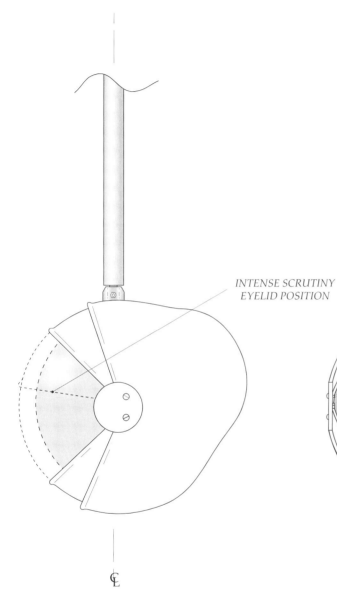

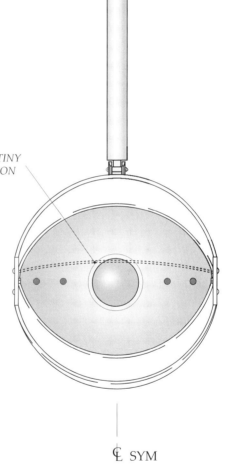

*INTENSE SCRUTINY
EYELID POSITION*

℄

PROFILE

℄ SYM

FRONT ELEVATION

project: Prisoner
(the no 6 file)

evidence

PROJECT: Prisoner

Number 6

One of the Village's recent procurements is Number 6. Much is known regarding this prisoner, the most important being that he is a paragon requiring utmost caution in handling. He may be an 'NP-complete' problem. The following regulations come from the Illuminati and are to be obeyed without question.

 Any procedures, experimental or traditional must be approved by Number 2 beforehand.

 There must be absolutely no permanent physical or mental damage inflicted upon Number 6 at any time.

 In passing, he may also be referred to as "The Cipher", or "The Enigma". These terms must never be used in the presence of Number 6.

Statistics

Date of birth: (unavailable) *4:31 am March 19, 1928*
Height: 6 ft
Weight: 12 stone
Hair: Brown
Eyes: Light Blue
Blood Type: B Rh+ {Lewis^{a-b+}, NN}
Recent Signature: _____ **(unavailable)** _____
Shoe Size: 10
Marital Status: Engaged; fiancée: Janet Portland
Physical and Psychological Peculiarities:
- Mole on left wrist.
- Freckle on right side of nose.
- Never eats sweets.
- Rarely drinks (special occasions excepted).
- Drinks lemon tea - does not take sugar. (subject gave up sugar 4 years, 3 months ago on medical advice)
- Enjoys 2 eggs and bacon for breakfast.
- Right handed.
- Light sleeper.
- Uses tobacco in cigar and white cigarette forms.
- Quotes Shakespeare on occasion.

History

Subject has a very coloured history. He attended Ratcliffe College in his early life, and at the age of 15, top of his class in woodwork. He went on to become a bombardier during the last year of World War II, and was subsequently shot down and held as a P.O.W. at Stalag Luft III for a short time. Following the end of the war, he attended the Royal Military College of Science (RMCS) where he achieved very high marks across the board. After graduation he was recruited by the British Secret Service and served as an intelligence officer serving under Colonel Jamieson and Major Thorpe, attached to NATO. Number 6 is an Olympic class fencer and boxer. He is now a prisoner and resides in the Village. See the "Drake" files for complete synopsis and details of his missions during his tenure as a secret agent man.

Psychological Make-up

Subject shows great enthusiasm for his work. He is utterly devoted and loyal, yet he has undefined patriotism. Number 6 is stoical, and too audacious and stalwart for his own good, and certainly much too much for the good of the community. He has a strong sense of territory and individuality. He is extremely independent, and indefatigable, and may be an archetype. "Ladies in distress" may be his Achilles heel.

Known Code Names

Country	Code Name	Alpha-Numeric
France	Jacques Duval Pierre Cordon	BA-17
Germany	Friedrich Schmidt Schultz	ZP-85
England	Peter Smith John Drake	ZM-73
Canada	John White Uriel	PM-28

Key To His House

Above is the key to Number 6's house. It has been retained by the Illumiati until further notice.

(actual size)

ridge end
bifurcation
ridge
bifurcation
core
TYPICA

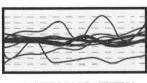
WAVEFORM PATTERN
(pronunciation of the word "you"

Thumb Print (right hand) and Voice Pattern

Above left is Number 6's right hand thumb print (loop pattern) and voice waveform pattern sample. They have been retained by the Illuminati and will not be returned.

Report On Number 6
(transcript from file: 'Crucible')

```
Normal Classification On Arrival.
Subject showed shock symptoms,
followed by accepted behaviour
pattern. Since then has been
uncooperative and distinctly
aggressive. Attempted to escape.
Subject proving exceptionally
difficult, but in view of his
importance, no extreme measures to be
used yet.
```

Number 6 - Residence (private)
Floor Plan

BATHING

SLEEPING

ROVER FRIENDLY
DOORWAY

RELAXATION

RISING WALL

ASCEND

LIVING

DESCEND

ASCEND

EATING

REFRIGERATION

LONDON HOME EXTENSION

project: prisoner

(the № 6 file)

Concealed Camera Locations
Number 6's Cottage
The cottage of Number 6 contains 17 concealed cameras.

The floor plans provided show the areas covered by each channel, as well as its parameters.

These cameras may be hidden in the walls, or may be of the embedded glass variety (see below for operational details). In the case of cameras that have pan / tilt capabilities and / or variable focal lengths, the entire pan (left to right, or right to left movement) and focal lengths (zoom in / out) is shown.

Embedded Glass Cameras
This is a special feature viewing system in the testing stage. Embedded in the glass of a television tube, window, or mirror, are crisscrossing fiber optic strands of varying thicknesses. The combination of strand diameters form a fixed focal length lens. The image focused from this lens is then fed through an optical cable to the receiving tube.

Concealed Camera Locations
Channels 1-4

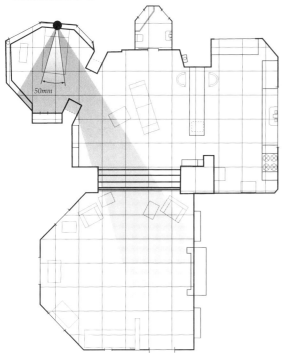

Channel 1
Focal Length Range: *fixed*
Default Focal Length: *50mm*
Pan / Tilt Enable: *YES*

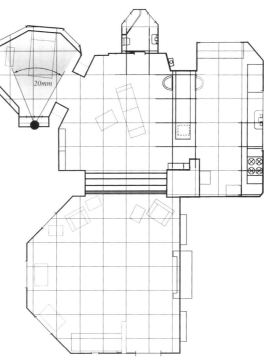

Channel 2
Focal Length Range: *fixed*
Default Focal Length: *20mm*
Pan / Tilt Enable: *NO*

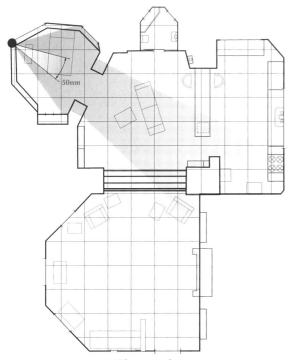

Channel 3
Focal Length Range: *18-86mm*
Default Focal Length: *50mm*
Pan / Tilt Enable: *YES*

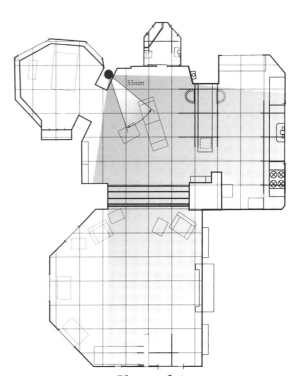

Channel 4
Focal Length Range: *12-120mm*
Default Focal Length: *35mm*
Pan / Tilt Enable: *YES*

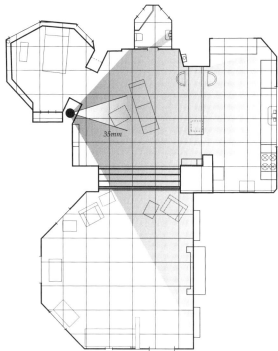

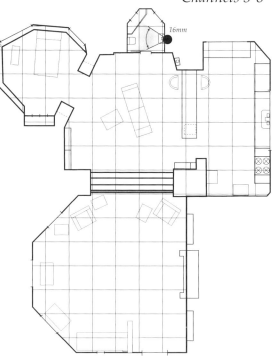

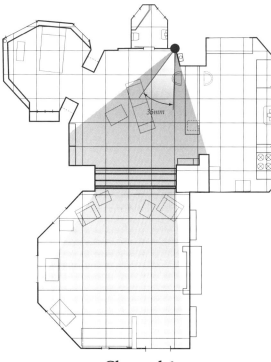

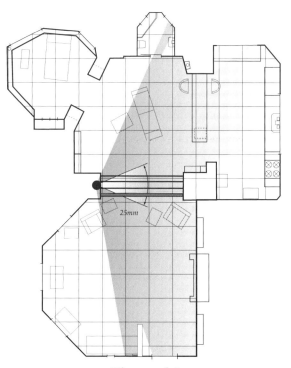

project: Prisoner

(the №6 file)

Channel 5
Focal Length Range: *12-120mm*
Default Focal Length: *35mm*
Pan / Tilt Enable: *YES*

Channel 6
Focal Length Range: *fixed*
Default Focal Length: *16mm*
Pan / Tilt Enable: *NO*

Channel 6
Focal Length Range: *12-120mm*
Default Focal Length: *35mm*
Pan / Tilt Enable: *YES*

Channel 8
Focal Length Range: *10-100mm*
Default Focal Length: *25mm*
Pan / Tilt Enable: *YES*

Concealed Camera Locations
Channels 9-12

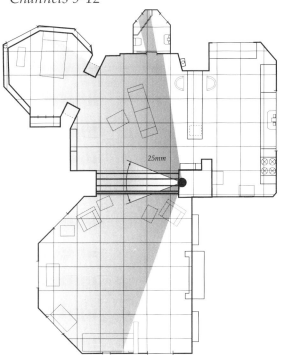

Channel 9
Focal Length Range: *10-100mm*
Default Focal Length: *25mm*
Pan / Tilt Enable: *YES*

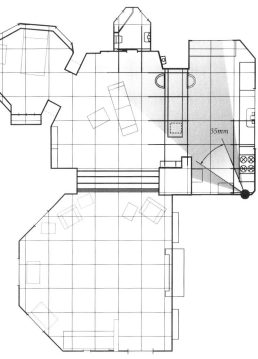

Channel 10
Focal Length Range: *12-120mm*
Default Focal Length: *35mm*
Pan / Tilt Enable: *YES*

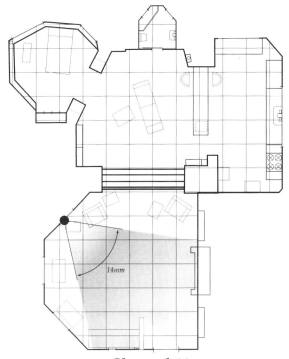

Channel 11
Focal Length Range: *fixed*
Default Focal Length: *14mm*
Pan / Tilt Enable: *NO*

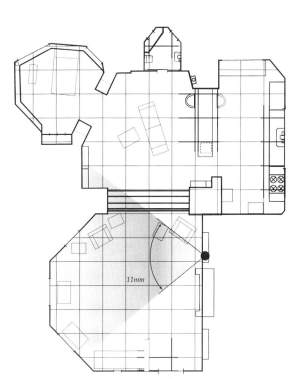

Channel 12
Focal Length Range: *fixed*
Default Focal Length: *11mm*
Pan / Tilt Enable: *NO*

project: Prisoner

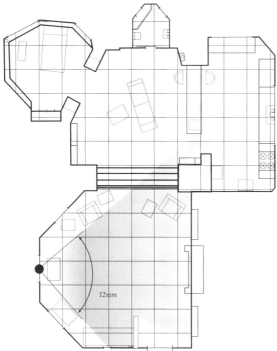

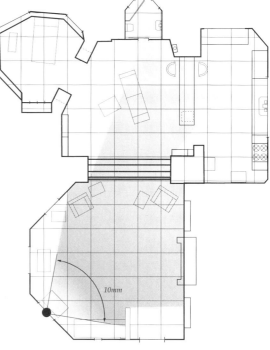

Channel 13
Focal Length Range: *fixed*
Default Focal Length: *12mm*
Pan / Tilt Enable: *NO*

Channel 14
Focal Length Range: *fixed*
Default Focal Length: *10mm*
Pan / Tilt Enable: *NO*

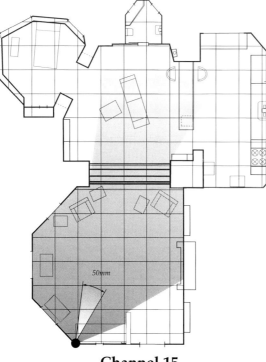

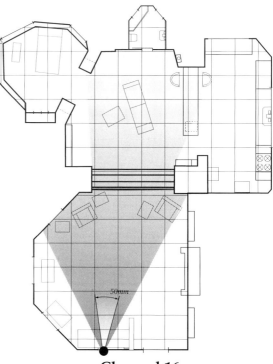

Channel 15
Focal Length Range: *9.5-95mm*
Default Focal Length: *50mm*
Pan / Tilt Enable: *YES*

Channel 16
Focal Length Range: *fixed*
Default Focal Length: *50mm*
Pan / Tilt Enable: *YES*

(the № 6 file)

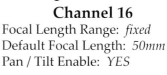

Concealed Camera Locations
Channel 2c, Channels Inclusive

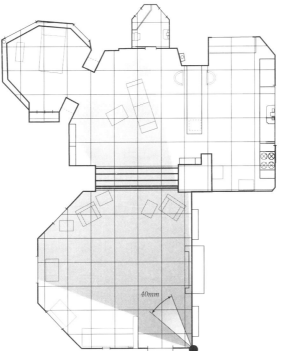

Channel 2c
Focal Length Range: *9.5-95mm*
Default Focal Length: *40mm*
Pan / Tilt Enable: *YES*

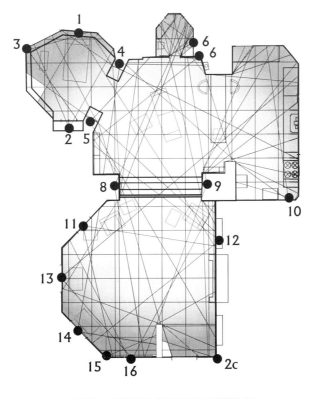

CHANNELS INCLUSIVE

project: prisoner

(the № 6 file)

surveillance photo ref# 300967/35498
subject: Number 6
location: cottage exterior

surveillance photo ref# 300967/0169
subject: Number 6
location: free sea

surveillance photo ref# 300967/38644
subject: Number 6
location: green dome

AUDIO TRANSCRIPTS

where am ı ?
ın the vıllage.
what do you want ?
ınformatıon.
whose sıde are you on ?
that would be tellıng.
we want ınformatıon, ınformatıon,
ınformatıon...
you won't get ıt.
by hook or by crook... we wıll.
who are you ?
the new number 2.
who ıs number 1 ?
you are number 6.
ı am not a number,
ı am a free man !

ı wıll not be pushed,
fıled, stamped, ındexed,
brıefed, debrıefed,
or numbered !
my lıfe ıs my **own.**

ı am not a number, ı am a
person. ın some place at
some tıme, all of you held
posıtıons of a secret nature
and had knowledge that was
ınvaluable to an enemy. lıke
me, you are here to have that
knowledge protected or
extracted. unlıke me many of
you have accepted the sıtuatıon
of your ımprısonment and wıll
dıe here lıke rotten cabbages.
the rest of you have gone over
to the sıde of our keepers.
whıch ıs whıch? how m
each? who's st⌐
you now?
wh

Lotus 7 —
General Arrangement

project: **Prisoner**

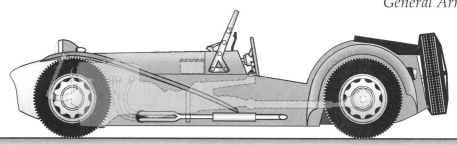

PROFILE

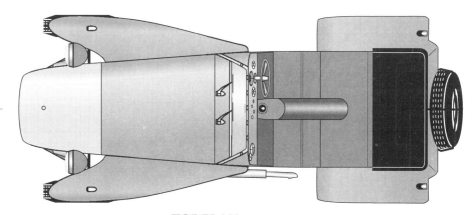

TOP PLAN

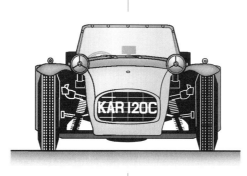

℄

FRONT ELEVATION

ENGINE SPEED (IN GEARS)

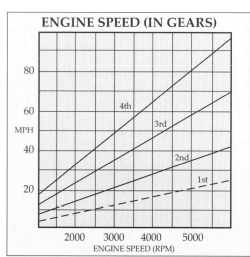

ACCELERATION AND COASTING

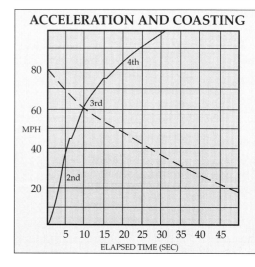

(the №6 file)

STATISTICS

Car Number:	*KAR 120C*
Chassis Number:	*17RD PR1*
Engine Number:	*461034TZ*
Maximum Speed:	*103.6 mph*
Manufacturer:	*(self built)*

personnel

Nomenclature

For official purposes, everyone has a number.
Below is a computerised printout of the
nomenclature list as of 05/09/66. Most numbers
are preassigned by the Illuminati, others are
assigned at the discretion of Number 2.

```
001 through 009 - High Level Villagers, to be treated with the
utmost courtesy, be they prisoners or warders.

001   Reserved.
002   Reserved (Village Chairman/Chief Administrator)
003   Special Case Prisoner.
004   Special Case Prisoner.
005   Special Case Prisoner.
006   Special Case Prisoner.
008   Special Case Prisoner.
009   Special Case Prisoner.

010-084   General level prisoners/warders/support personnel,
          including the Supervisor.

085-114   General Observers.

115-149   General level prisoners/warders/support personnel.

150-219   Guards.
          150-165   Shift 1.
          166-192   Shift 2.
          193-219   Reserve Force (Assembly Hall).

220-235   General level prisoners/warders/support personnel.

236-240   Prime Motive Observers.

241-284   Misc. Staff (Lab technicians/doctors/etc.)

285-291   Senior Observers (SeeSaw)
          285-286   Shift 1.
          288-289   Shift 2.
          290-291   Shift 3.

292-302   Subsidiary Personnel (Control Room Post Observers)
          292-296   Shift 1.
          298-302   Shift 2.
```

—Badge
Detail Arrangement

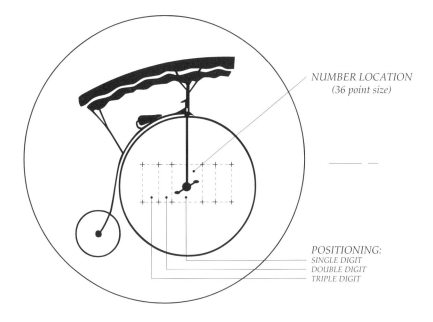

NUMBER LOCATION
(36 point size)

POSITIONING:
SINGLE DIGIT
DOUBLE DIGIT
TRIPLE DIGIT

℄L

(shown actual size)

ALTERNATE DESIGN

PRACTICAL

TYPEFACE

012345689

Personnel—

Identification Cards (photostat plate imprints)

personnel

No.

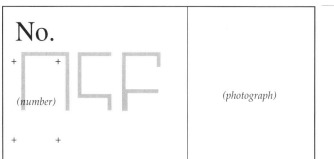

+   +

(number)

+   +

(photograph)

CARD OF IDENTITY

+   +

(number)

+   +

health to
bε
rεnewed
εach month

HEALTH AND WELFARE CARD

1	2	3	4	5	6		8

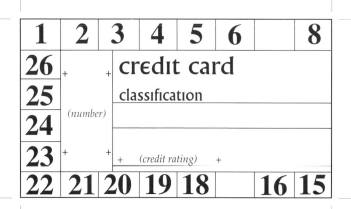

26	+	+	credit card
25			classification
24	*(number)*		
23	+	+	+ *(credit rating)* +

22	21	20	19	18		16	15

CREDIT CARD

+   *(position)*   +

+   +

+   *(employment rating)*   +

(number)

+   +

+   *(advancement potential)*   +

EMPLOYMENT CARD

9d

the village files

— Clothing
Male / Female

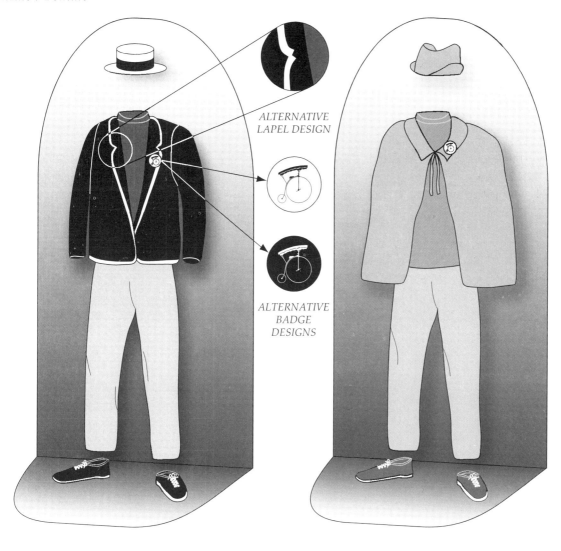

ALTERNATIVE
LAPEL DESIGN

ALTERNATIVE
BADGE
DESIGNS

MALE

FEMALE

MALE / FEMALE - SWEATER

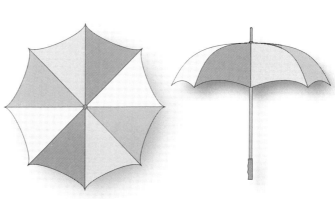

UMBRELLA

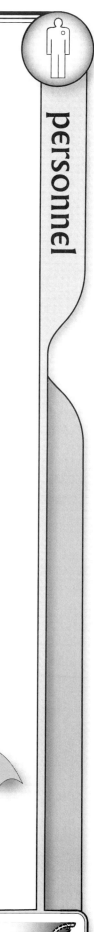

personnel

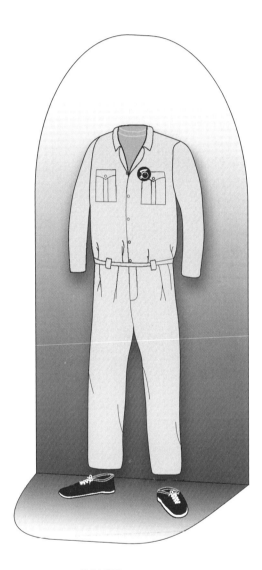

MALE

FEMALE

—Clothing
Doctor / Kosho

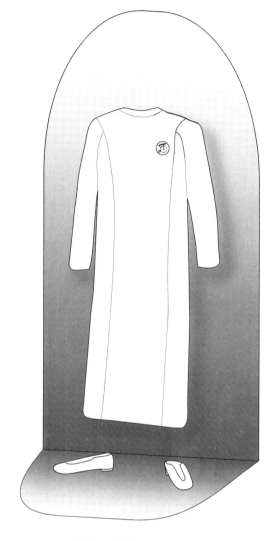

DOCTOR

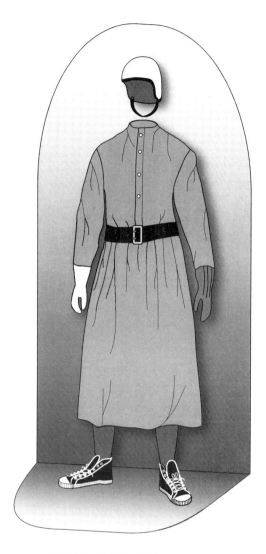

KOSHO FATIGUES

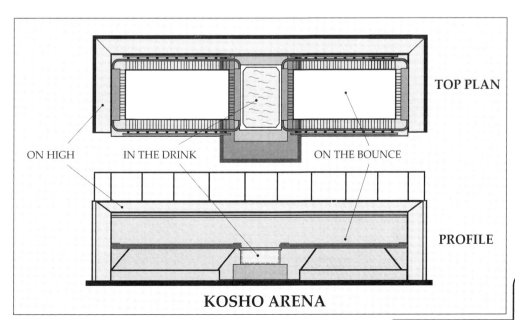

TOP PLAN

ON HIGH   IN THE DRINK   ON THE BOUNCE

PROFILE

KOSHO ARENA

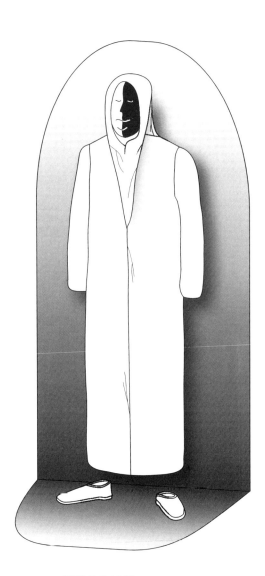

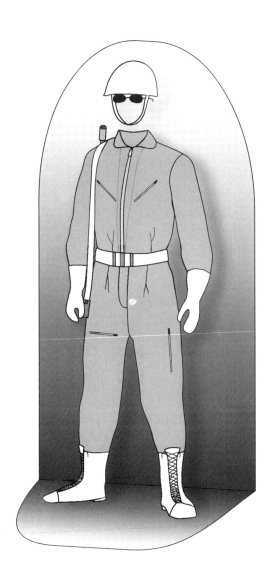

DELEGATE

GUARD

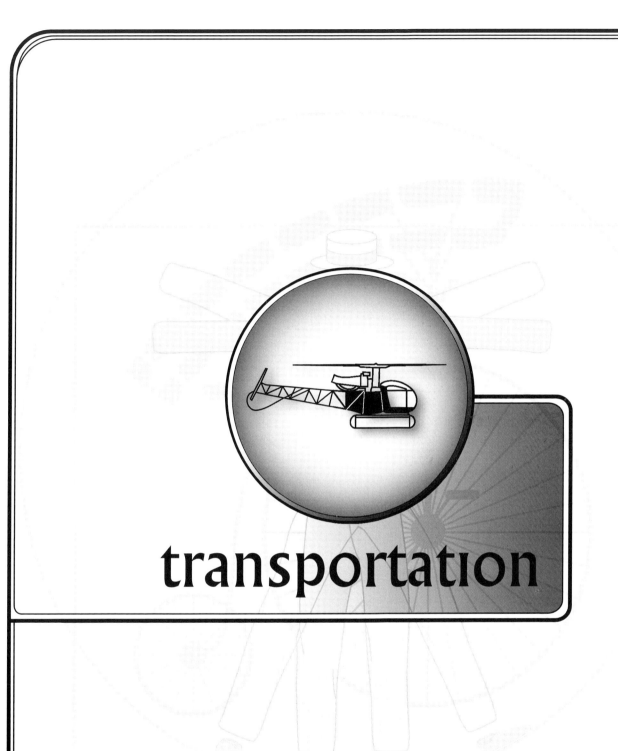

transportation

transportation

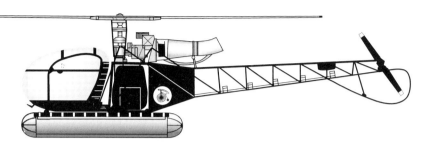

PROFILE

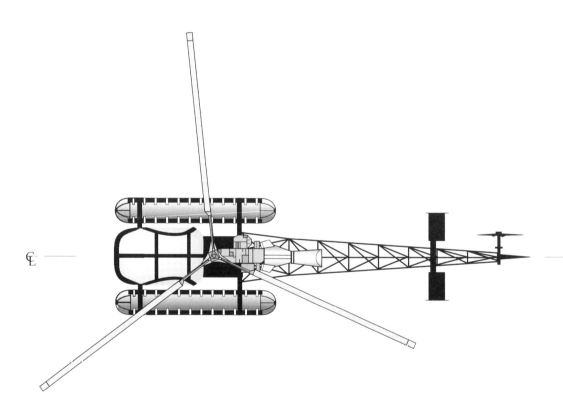

C̵L

TOP PLAN

STATISTICS

Type:	*VILLAGE ISSUE ALOUETTE II*
Capacity:	*2 villagers + cargo*
Service Ceiling	*10,500 feet*
Hovering Ceiling:	*6,600 feet*
Range:	*450 miles*
Maximum Speed:	*200 mph*

—Taxi
General Arrangement

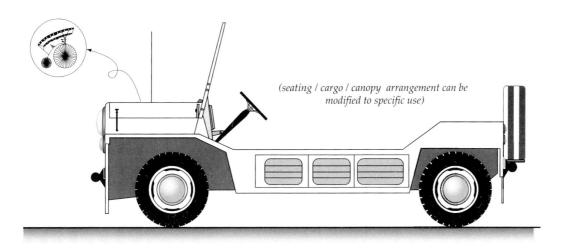

(seating / cargo / canopy arrangement can be modified to specific use)

PROFILE

taxi

₵

FRONT ELEVATION

STATISTICS

Type:	*VILLAGE TAXI / ALL-PURPOSE VEHICLE*
Capacity:	*4 villagers*
Maximum Speed:	*40 mph*

Tractor—
General Arrangement

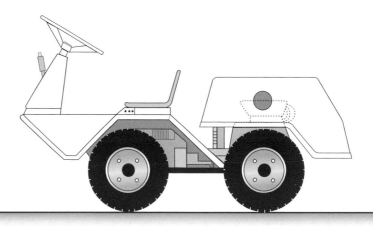

PROFILE

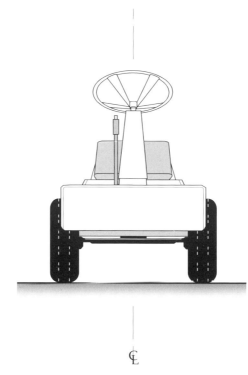

℄

FRONT ELEVATION

STATISTICS

Type:	*VILLAGE ISSUE TRACTOR*
Capacity:	*1 villager*
Maximum Speed:	*1/2 mph*

In The Event Of An Emergency Driver Is Permitted To Walk

transportation

SpeedBoat
General Arrangement

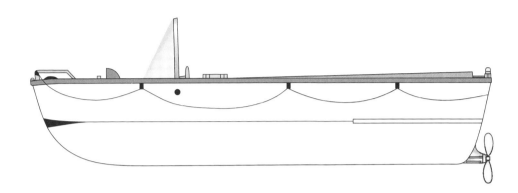

PROFILE

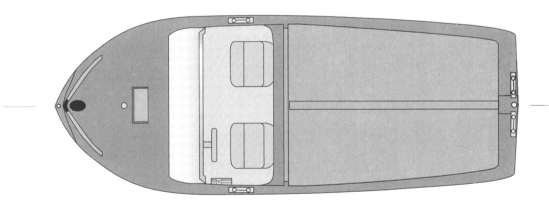

TOP PLAN

STATISTICS

Type:	*VILLAGE ISSUE SPEEDBOAT*
Capacity:	*2 villagers + cargo*
Maximum Speed:	*52 knots*

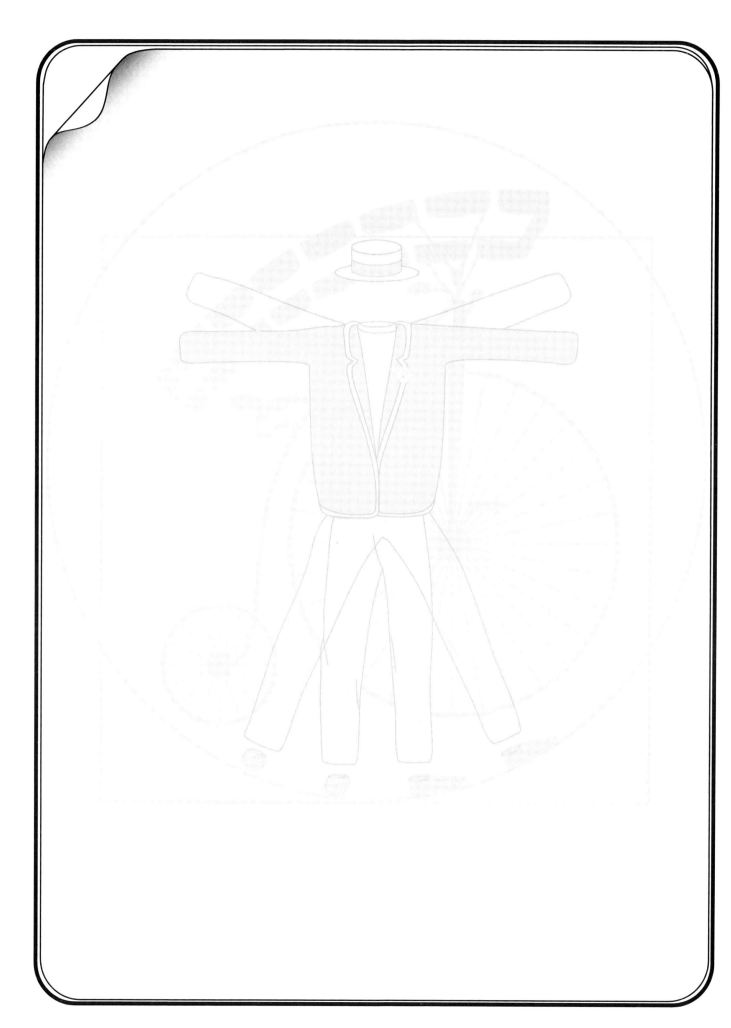

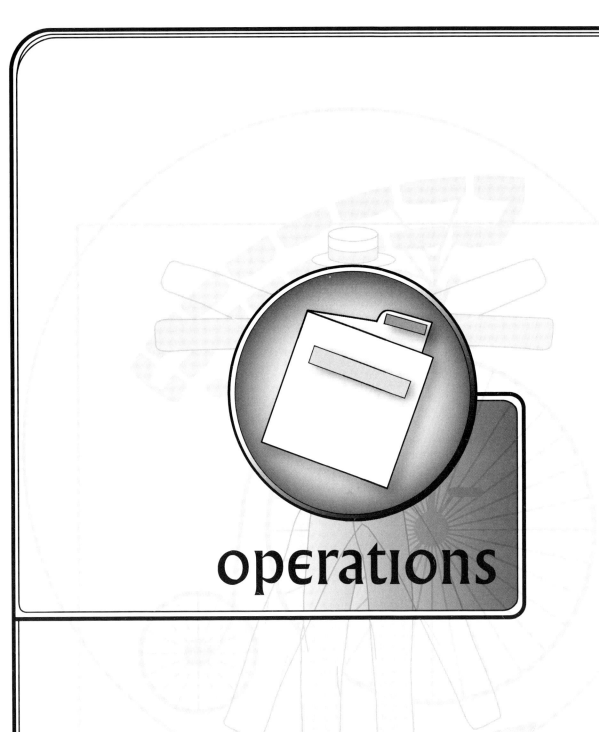

operations

operations

Operational Divisions
The following operational divisions are referred to as "Plan Division (A - Z)".

A
B
C
D
E
F
G
H
I
J
K
L

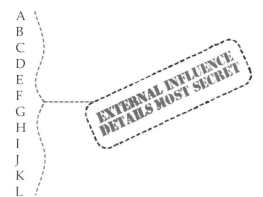

EXTERNAL INFLUENCE
DETAILS MOST SECRET

M - Internal Influence
    (Scientific Experimentation)
N - Internal Influence - Special Services
    (Embryo Room, Assembly Hall, etc.)
O - Internal Influence - Anti-Jammer Warders
P - Internal Influence - Town Council
Q - Internal Influence - Covert Operatives
R - Resuscitation Specialists
S - Assembly Hall Delegates
T - Public Minded Citizens (PMC's)
U - Pantheon Specialists
V - Launch Crews
W
X
Y
Z

DEVOTED TO
SPECIAL CASE PRISONERS

Select Operations List
Operation "Windscale" (Plan Division E)
See also Program "Vela Uniform" (Plan Division C),
and Projects "Longshot", "Milgrow", "Cannikin",
"Faultless", "Sedan Crater", "Sterling", et al; cold and
warm weather environments.

Situation "FallOut"
Contingency plans for this unlikely event are as
follows:

1) Contact control room.
2) Declaration of Red Alert.
3) Complete evacuation of all Village personnel.
4) Shutdown of Village electrical power.
5) Deflagration of Village and surrounding area.
6) Confirmation of plausible deniability stability.

Operation "Zircon"
Operation Zircon will consist of the clandestine
placement of "Zircon Spy" satellites in
geostationary orbit. These satellites are planned
to complement and enhance the Village's already
existing global spy network. (Plan Division G)

Plan "Maelstrom"
This plan is in effect if and when Situation FallOut
occurs, and Assembly Hall roof retraction is not
initiated.

Special Projects and Operations List (partial)

Operation Ajax	Operation Ivy Bells
Operation Anadyr	Operation Jennifer
Project Andromeda	Operation Lamia
Operation Aurora	Project Libra
Project Aurora	Operation Luminaire
Project Blossom	Operation Majestic (MJ-12)
Operation Bluebell	Operation Malpas
Operation Boot	Operation Mamba
Project Calaway	Project MKULTRA
Project Capricorn	Operation Mongoose
Operation Chaos	Project Magnet
Operation Choir	Project Mogul
Operation Clickbeetle	Operation Paperclip
Operation Codford	Operation Pennyfarthing
Project Cooler	Operation Permindex
Operation Corona	Operation Phoenix
Operation DESOTO	Project Pisces
Operation Dinar	Operation Price Of Peace
Directive 17	Operation Price of Power
Operation Downfall	Project Prisoners of Power
Project Echelon	Project Protect Other People
Project ECOMCON	Operation Quicksilver
Operation Engulf	Plan R
Operation Epsilon	Program Rivet Joint
Project Galileo	Operation Sapphire
Project Garnet	Program Satyr
Project Gemini	Project SHAD
Program Genetrix	Project Sign
Operation Gideon	Operation Silver
Project Gnome	Project Silverbug
Operation Gold	Operation Solo
Operation Grillflame	Operation Stockade
Project Grudge	Project Tempest
Operation Harbrink	Operation Tophat
Operation Hexagon	Project Umbra
Plan Huston	Program Vela Uniform
Project Icecap	Project Venona
Operation Ichthyic	Project XA

Prisoner Specific Operations List (partial)
Operation A, B, and C (ABC)
Operation Conundrum (CONUND)
Operation Crucible (CRU)
Operation Dead Dance (DD)
Operation Finish All (FIN)
Operation Free All (FREE)
Operation Many Happy Returns (MHR)
Project Prisoner (PRIS)
Operation Schizoid (SCHIZ)
    (see also 'Juxtaposition Reciprocity')
Plan Vanguard (VANG)

miscellaneous

Currency

Currency works on a credit system. A credit
card is issued to all prisoners showing their
available work units that can be exchanged for
goods and services. Below is a partial list.

Item	Product / Service	Credit Units
Taxi ride (local only)	S	2 maximum
Phone call (local only)	S	free
Tally Ho	P	2
Coffee	P	2 per cup
Map (black and white)	P	4
Map (colour)	P	10
Notebook	P	3
Adhesive tape	P	5 per roll
Cuckoo clock	P	39
Each 3 words in a Tally Ho private note	S	1
Vodka (non-alcoholic)	P	16 per bottle
Whiskey (non-alcoholic)	P	24 per bottle
Scotch (non-alcoholic)	P	24 per bottle
Repair services	S	free
Bag of sweets	P	1
1st prize in an art competition	*	2000

Scriptures
The following are the scriptures of the Prototype: Village
facility. They are to be used as often as possible.

a still tongue makes a happy life
be seeing you
ending is better than mending
feel free
humour is the essential ingredient of a democratic society
individuals are all the same
judgment is the mirror
music makes a quiet mind
music begins where words leave off
music says all
of the people, by the people, for the people
questions are a burden to others; answers, a prison for oneself
suspicion breeds confidence
trust, but verify
truth is a triple edged sword
walk on the grass

miscellaneous

your

namɛ

hɛrɛ

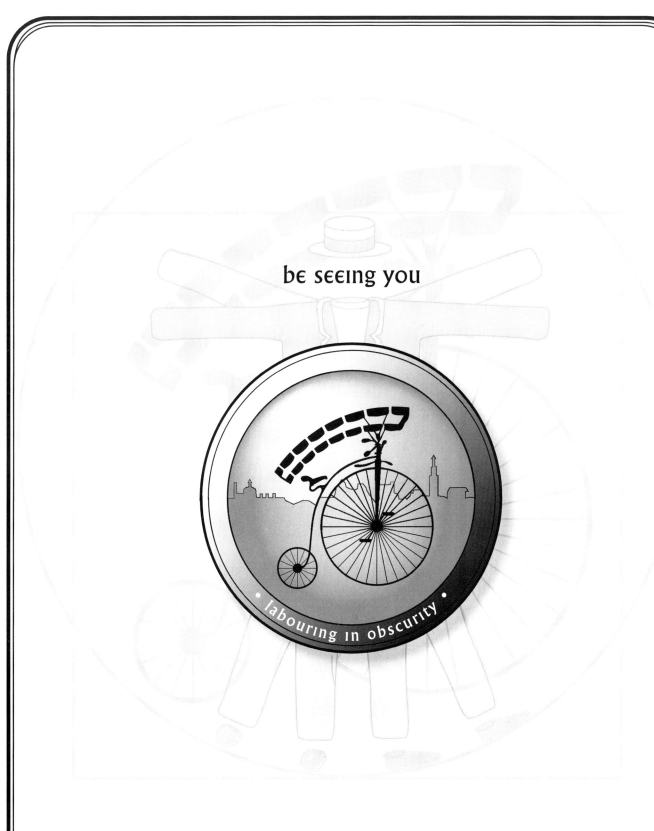

be seeing you

labouring in obscurity

Tally Ho Publishings - 1967

This manual is listed under Tally Ho
Publishings which is a short arm member of
Your Established Village Community.